How Should Democracies Fight Terrorism?

Political Theory Today

Patti Tamara Lenard

How Should Democracies Fight Terrorism?

polity

The right of Patti Tamara Lenard to be identified as Author of this Work has been asserted in accordance with the UK Copyright, Designs and Patents Act 1988.

First published in 2020 by Polity Press

Polity Press
65 Bridge Street
Cambridge CB2 1UR, UK

Polity Press
101 Station Landing
Suite 300
Medford, MA 02155, USA

ISBN-13: 978-1-5095-4075-4
ISBN-13: 978-1-5095-4076-1 (pb)

A catalogue record for this book is available from the British Library.

Library of Congress Cataloging-in-Publication Data
Names: Lenard, Patti Tamara, 1975- author.
Title: How should democracies fight terrorism? / Patti Tamara Lenard.
Description: Cambridge, UK ; Medford, MA : Polity Press, 2020. | Series:
    Political theory today | Includes bibliographical references. | Summary:
    "Why our democratic values shouldn't be sacrificed on the altar of
    national security"-- Provided by publisher.
Identifiers: LCCN 2020000160 | ISBN 9781509540754 (hardback) | ISBN
    9781509540761 (paperback) | ISBN 9781509540778 (epub)
Subjects: LCSH: Terrorism--Prevention--Moral and ethical aspects. |
    Democracy--Moral and ethical aspects.
Classification: LCC HV6431 .L456 2020 | DDC 363.325/16--dc23
LC record available at https://lccn.loc.gov/2020000160

Typeset in 11 on 15 Sabon by Servis Filmsetting Ltd, Stockport, Cheshire
Printed and bound in Great Britain by CPI Group (UK) Ltd, Croydon

For further information on Polity, visit our website: politybooks.com

Contents

Acknowledgments

I began drafting the text that turned into this book while visiting the University of Toronto's Centre for Ethics in early 2019, and I am very grateful to the welcoming faculty and students there. Margaret Moore and David Miller read early drafts and I am indebted to them for their critical comments. Peter Balint read and offered comments on chapter 3 when I was feeling especially unsatisfied with it. The earliest of my work on questions of security was done in collaboration with my colleague Wesley Wark, who read a late version of the manuscript and offered the critical suggestions that only an expert in national security can do. The original account of the security test was developed in collaboration with Terry Macdonald, in an article published in *Perspectives on Politics*. Three reviewers for Polity Press, and George Owers and Julia

Davies, offered wonderfully helpful comments on the manuscript. Finally, my partner-in-all-things, Jacob Krich, read and commented on the first version of this manuscript, and most of the last, and never (ever) tired of going through each detail of the argument with me. There are no words adequate to thank him for all that he has done, and continues every day to do, for me and the sweet family that we are building together.

Introduction

States around the world are striving to protect their citizens from terrorism. Democratic states have an additional struggle in this task because not only must they protect their citizens from terrorism, they must do so in ways that respect and protect their rights. The challenge of combatting terrorism is complicated, further, by the myriad forms that terrorism takes. Consider the following cases.

In 2016, the Islamic State in Syria and Iraq (ISIS) took credit for Mohamed Lahouaiej-Bouhlel's decision to drive a 19-tonne cargo truck into a crowd of people celebrating Bastille Day in Nice, France, killing nearly 90 people. Lahouaiej-Bouhlel was killed at the scene of the crime, but after-the-fact investigations suggested he had been radicalized online, where he had expressed interest in and sympathy with ISIS violence.

In 2017, Sufiyan Mustafa was stripped of his British citizenship while he was in Syria, and he was denied the right to return to the United Kingdom. He is accused by the British government of fighting with ISIS, a claim that he denies, arguing in fact, that he fought on the side of a group that was being supported with American and British weapons. He claims that he is being tainted by the crimes of his father, Abu Hamza al-Masri, who is serving a life sentence for terrorist crimes in the United States. Mustafa has requested to return to the United Kingdom to make the case in a British court that he is not a terrorist; but, with the revocation of his citizenship, his right to make this case has effectively been extinguished.

In late 2018, a man yelling "All Jews must die" entered a synagogue during Saturday morning Sabbath services, in Pittsburgh, Pennsylvania, and shot and killed 11 people. Online, and prior to the shooting, Robert Bowers had posted a series of anti-Semitic comments, directed mainly at the Hebrew Immigrant Aid Society, accusing it of supporting the movement of irregular migrants into the United States. His online posting history suggests a commitment to far-right extremism, and his comments targeted Jews and African Americans, referring to both groups using a range of common slurs.

Similarly, the Australian migrant to New Zealand[1] who entered two separate mosques and murdered 51 Muslims in 2019 had posted a manifesto online before undertaking this crime, citing his hatred of immigrants and Muslims; and Patrick Wood Crusius, who entered a Walmart in El Paso, Texas in 2019 and murdered 22 people, had posted a manifesto online citing his hatred of Hispanics, and immigrants more generally, claiming that they were responsible for the dilution of the white race.

These examples showcase two forms of terrorism that are occupying the attention of democratic security authorities: terrorism committed by so-called "far-right extremists," as in the case of Bowers, Crusius, and the gunman in New Zealand; and terrorism committed in the name of violent religious extremism, as in the case of Lahouaiej-Bouhlel and, allegedly, Mustafa. These two forms of terrorism have much in common, and also much that makes them distinct. This book focuses on how democratic states can be both fair and effective as they combat the threats posed by both types of terrorism.

---

[1] Following the attacks on the mosques in New Zealand, Prime Minister Jacinda Ardern declared her refusal to speak the name of the terrorist in public, which this text respects.

What Is Terrorism?

Among scholars of terrorism, there is considerable disagreement about how to define terrorist organizations and terrorist actions. Terrorist actors are sometimes states – as was Nazi Germany – or, more often, sub-state organizations such as the Irish Republican Army (IRA) and Euskadi Ta Askatasuna (ETA) (Peonidis 2004, 321). Usually, terrorist organizations have recognizably political objectives, which serve to distinguish terrorist acts from pointless or criminal killing. These political ends can be expansive, including subjugating populations, overthrowing colonial or otherwise oppressive rulers, and destroying unjust economic regimes; or they can be narrow – for example, a demand that prisoners be released. The possession of a recognizably political objective suggests, at least in principle, that a political settlement of some kind can end terrorism.

Crucially, to achieve their objectives, terrorists act by generating fear or anxiety among a population (Scheffler 2006, 6; Townshend 2002, 15). This fear is often generated by carrying out a violent action, especially one that carries with it a "credible threat of repeated attacks" (Steinhoff 2007, 120; Coady 1985).

Finally, terrorism often targets innocent civilians

on a relatively random basis, though there are disa-greements about what renders a civilian innocent of, or complicit in, whatever harms the terrorists are intending to combat or highlight by their actions (Townshend 2002, 8; Steinhoff 2007, 112–17). There are often exceptions to this latter feature, however – the IRA, for example, has sometimes claimed to aim at restricting its violence to those it believed were actively working on behalf of the British state.

To summarize, for the purposes of this book, terrorist organizations are those that: (1) possess a recognizably political objective, which (2) they attempt to achieve by engaging in actions aimed at inducing widespread anxiety and fear in particular by (3) perpetrating violence against innocents and credibly threatening to perpetrate more. Skeptical readers might believe that violent religious extrem-ism and far-right extremist violence are not much like terrorism in the past, but in fact, as the rest of this introduction suggests, they meet all of these key requirements.

It is important to distinguish between the stated objectives of terrorist organizations and the tactics they deploy. Terrorist tactics vary considerably, including targeted assassinations, shooting ram-pages, hostage-taking, planting of bombs in public spaces, driving of trucks into crowded spaces, suicide bombings and hijacking of planes. In some cases, the objectives pursued by terrorists may be recognized as legitimate, even where their tactics are not. When opponents of apartheid in South Africa engaged in "necklacing," the placing of rubber tires dipped in gasoline around the neck of opponents and setting them on fire, many observers deplored the practice as terrorism, even as they supported the objective of dismantling apartheid. Similarly, many people support the objective of a United Ireland, even as they agree that labelling the IRA "terrorist" is appropriate. In others, it may be that both the objectives and the tactics of terrorists are condemned, as they were in the case of Nazi Germany's objective to rid Germany (and the world) of Jews.

For the last several decades, and certainly in heightened form since 9/11, the popular image of a terrorist is that of a young Middle Eastern man, like Lahouaiej-Bouhlel, who harbors hostility toward the values that define democratic states. The danger he represents – of violent religious extremism, much of it connected to ISIS – has been the focus of much recent terrorism prevention policy-making. The danger posed by far-right extremism, however, is just as significant in democratic states, is growing, and until recently has appeared to be taken less seriously. In the United States, for example, between 2009 and 2018, 73 percent of lethal attacks labelled terrorism were committed by far-right extremists, whereas only 23 percent were committed by violent religious extremists (Serwer 2019). The same is true worldwide, where the crimes committed by far-right extremists far outpace those committed in the name of violent religious extremism (Strickland 2019). Mark Rowley, former head of the London Metropolitan Police's counter-terrorism unit, stated publicly in 2018 that, in his view, the UK was paying insufficient attention to the growing threat posed by far-right extremism: "I don't think we've woken up to it enough . . . it's significant and growing, and what I've seen over the last couple of years is a lack of recognition of that" (Busby 2018).

Both violent religious extremism and far-right extremism intend to instill fear, by committing horrific crimes against innocents, in the hopes that the resultant fear and anxiety will undermine the state's capacities to provide the goods that citizens expect. What differs is only the targets of violence. Far-right extremists are typically targeting minority or disadvantaged groups, including religious, ethnic or cultural minorities, as well as women or sexual minorities. In the case of the New Zealand mosque attacks, or Alexandre Bisonnette's attacks on a mosque in Quebec, Canada, or in Robert Bowers' attack on Jews, the intent was to instill fear in members of particular groups – insofar as they are members of identifiable groups – rather than society at large. Religious extremists often target, simply, "infidels," though sometimes they target individuals or groups who are believed to be more directly responsible for military actions in the Middle East, or for propagating hatred against Muslims. British soldier Lee Rigby was targeted by religious extremists for his participation in British military actions in the Middle East, for example, and *Charlie Hebdo* employees were targeted for the magazine's contentious portrayals of the prophet Mohammed, and Islam more generally.

The objectives pursued by far-right extremists and violent religious extremists are sometimes thought to be hard to discern. It is sometimes difficult to identify the political objectives of those carrying out truck attacks or stabbings, and post-crime evaluations often involve sifting through private correspondence and internet activity to identify the possible motives of such terrorist actors. In the case of far-right extremist crimes, the label of "far-right" extremist is applied after the fact, in response to the discovery of (usually online) statements of hatred for minorities whose presence, the perpetrator believed, was diluting or undermining something of alleged importance. In the case of violent religious extremists, objectives are sometimes to cause the withdrawal of western intervention in the Middle East, sometimes to contribute to the construction of an Islamic caliphate in parts of Syria and Iraq, and sometimes simply to kill so-called "infidels" in the name of a larger putatively religious objective. Regardless of how the objectives are understood, it is widely agreed that the tactics pursued, by both parties, are recognizably terrorist: they aim to create anxiety and fear among a population by harming innocents, "with the aim of degrading the social order and reducing its capacity to support a flourishing social life" (Scheffler 2006, 6). The intention to create *fear* will be central to the book's arguments with respect to how best to punish terrorists.

As noted earlier, an act of terrorism is one that creates terror, at least in part, by generating credible threats of future harm. Historically, the source of this credible threat stemmed from individual terrorists' connections to a larger organization with the structure and resources to continue terrorizing, even if a particular perpetrator was captured or killed. In the cases of violent religious and far right extremists, however, the actors are often alleged to be loners who are radicalized by, or even simply inspired by, others with similar views. Such lone actors hardly constitute a terrorist *movement* or *organization*, with the capacity to credibly threaten future harm, one might say. As the spread of both violent religious extremism and far-right extremism continues, however, it is clear enough that there exists a loose network of individuals with roughly similar views and objectives, motivated by radical ideologies that are inspiring similar actions for overlapping reasons. This loose network provides the credible threat of further violence, even in the absence of a central planner. ISIS itself has at times behaved more like historical terrorist organizations, recruiting and mobilizing fighters in ways that are analogous to the IRA or ETA, even though much recent terrorism enacted in its name has been conducted by radicalized individuals without direct ISIS planning of, or involvement in, their attacks. Similarly, far-right extremists usually find inspiration and support from online communities – including, for example, Reddit, 8chan and 8kun – that propagate the ideology that feeds their hatred and anger. The mechanisms by which new terrorists are born and groomed may have changed in the last 20 years, but their goals have not.

Outline of the Book

This book considers how democratic states should punish and prevent terrorism – both violent religious extremism and far-right extremism – in diverse democratic states that are characterized by inequalities that often follow racial, ethnic and cultural lines. Both of these types of terrorism raise difficult practical and moral questions about how democracies can and should treat citizens who have committed, or are believed to be intending to commit, terrorist crimes, internally and abroad. This book describes the principles that should guide and frame the way in which security authorities in democratic states protect citizens from terrorism within their jurisdiction. These are, at their most basic, principles intended to protect the equality of all citizens in democratic states, usually in the form of a robust set of rights.

Fighting terrorism is a multi-stranded, global exercise, and this book cannot assess all the tools that democratic states possess to do so, nor all the ways in which they ought to contribute to what is in many ways a global effort. Moreover, it bears noting at the outset that the vast, vast, majority of terrorist incidents do not take place in the democratic countries that are the focus of this book; globally, in 2017, fewer than 2 percent of deaths from terrorism took place in Europe, North America and Australia / New Zealand (Ritchie et al. 2019). To constrain the focus even further, this book is centrally focused on how democracies should treat *citizens*, who are accused of terrorism or of having terrorist sympathies; democracies have special duties to their citizens, including those who are victims of crimes, those who commit them, and those who expect to be protected from them. Rather than focus on how and when democracies should join fights against terrorism abroad, and how they should behave as contributors to the global fight against terrorism, this book considers domestic policy with respect to: (1) fair *punishments* for terrorist crimes, committed at home and abroad; and (2) fair mechanisms for *preventing* terrorist crimes, committed at home and abroad.

Chapter 1 begins with an articulation of what security is and why it is important. It then focuses on the most common way in which democratic states have grappled with terrorism-fighting policies – namely, in terms of the security–rights debate. As many political theorists and political actors have conceived it, modern-day terrorism is such a grave threat that citizens and residents are now forced into hard choices: they must sacrifice *either* their security *or* their rights. According to some scholars, if states are to be truly serious about protecting the national security of citizens and residents, some rights – especially speech, movement and privacy rights – must be sacrificed. According to others, the rights to which citizens are entitled must be treated as sacrosanct, and, correspondingly, policies that undercut them – even in the name of security – are to be rejected. The chapter proposes that both sides of this debate make important errors and proposes an alternative way forward, focused on protecting the equality that is supposed to be foundational to democratic accounts of citizenship. This argument requires a rearticulation and expansion of the conceptual core of security, so that it is treated as a feature of both individuals and communities – as will be seen, the protection of these can sometimes press in different policy directions.

Chapter 2 focuses on how states should punish citizens who, by their criminal actions, aim to terrorize fellow citizens. It details the moral questions raised by the two classes of cases of terrorism outlined above: violent religious extremism and far-right extremism. The chapter applies the equality-based account of security that is developed in chapter 1 to assess the appropriate ways in which punishment for terrorist crimes should be meted out. It argues that an emphasis on *rehabilitation* and *communication* are essential components of any punishment in a democratic state – any punishment that is fair provides a road by which criminals, even terrorist-criminals, can return to full and equal standing in democratic states. It argues, correspondingly, that sentencing enhancements for terrorist crimes and hate crimes are both consistent with a commitment to the full and equal standing of citizens, and attentive to the gravity of terrorist crimes, but that revoking the citizenship of those who are suspected or convicted of terrorist crimes is not. In general, this chapter is motivated by the observation that a democracy is in part judged by how fairly it treats those who are believed to have – and who, in fact, have – done *wrong*.

Chapter 3 focuses on the mechanisms by which states *prevent* terrorist crimes. There are many preventative strategies a state may adopt, which target communities that are said to harbor terrorists and individuals who are believed to be more likely to commit terrorist acts. The chapter begins by outlining a "security test," to permit the moral evaluation of specific preventative policies. In brief, the test requires that a policy be genuinely connected to the protection of security; that the costs it imposes on citizens are assessed and judged to be proportionate to the benefits they are supposed to generate; and that the justifications for a policy, and its implementation, are made transparent. This test can therefore permit the adoption of counter-terrorism strategies with disproportionate impact on some communities; it also highlights that any policy with such an impact must meet a high burden of proof. Meeting this burden requires that real evidence is provided of a policy's necessity and its efficacy; in particular, where the burdens fall heavily on a racial or religious minority that already struggles to exercise its rights on an equal basis, evidence must be furnished that other, less costly, policies cannot accomplish the sought-after objective.

This test is then applied to three forms of terror ism prevention: policies that expand the domain of prohibited speech in an attempt to reduce the capacity of terrorists to encourage and support violence; policies that restrict the movement of citizens who are suspected of desiring to travel abroad to join terrorist cells; and policies that permit the surveillance of communities that are believed to harbor terrorists, as well as individuals who are believed to be at risk of committing terrorist acts. Policies that expand the domain of prohibited speech impact all citizens of a jurisdiction equally, but the others – those that restrict movement and those that permit surveillance – usually engage in the selection of specific targets. So, chapter 3 also considers what renders this selection fair. In so doing, it considers the legitimacy of profiling possible targets, including by race. Contextual factors will often press against the use of racial profiling, even in cases where evidence suggests doing so will produce a (light) security benefit.

A worry running through the book is that the battles against certain forms of terrorism have created conditions under which the equal protection of the citizenship rights of many – mainly minority – citizens is at risk. In some cases, political actors have stoked fears of terrorism for political gain, efforts which appear to give legitimacy to anti-Muslim prejudice, and which appear to have increased incidents of violence and discrimination against Muslim and Muslim-appearing individuals (e.g., Ivandic et al. 2019). Correspondingly, it argues that any justified counter-terrorism effort in a democratic state – whether it be with respect to punishing terrorists or with respect to preventing them – must direct special attention to protecting the rights of minority citizens. Doing so is central to protecting their trust in, and collaboration with, the wide-ranging counter-terrorism measures adopted in democratic states.

1

Security, Rights and Equality

This book opened with recent examples of terrorism, all of which are aimed at undermining the security of citizens of democratic states. The general response to these attacks has been a call for greater security, often via policies that constrain (that is, limit the scope of) or restrict (that is, deny) the exercise of some key democratic rights. After the truck attack in Nice, there were calls for greater surveillance, for which citizens of France were asked to sacrifice some privacy. After Anders Breivik shot and killed nearly 70 people participating in a summer camp associated with a political party he detested (one he believed was responsible for admitting the Muslims he believed were a scourge in Europe), there were calls for greater infiltration of internet spaces known to support and mobilize those with far-right views, one consequence of which might be restricted access to platforms in which to exercise hateful speech. What these examples highlight is a common framework for understanding the choices that democratic states are said to confront: to fight terror, democratic states must choose between protecting national security and protecting civil rights. In the most common way of expressing this choice, security must be balanced against rights, and the goal is to find the best balance between them (Newey 2012; Reed 2013). The supposed best balance often translates into a priority for security since – say many national security authorities – rights are of no use if it is unsafe to use them.

However, this chapter argues, the idea that political actors in an era of terrorism are just tasked with finding the appropriate balance between "security" and "rights" is too simple to help adjudicate the difficult cases with which this chapter began. Instead, it proposes two modifications in order to better assess the challenges democratic states face in combatting terrorism. First, security must be understood to have an individual ("I am secure") and collective ("the city of Ottawa is secure") dimension. Second, democratic states may face situations in which a community can overall be more secure only if the rights of all – or only some – citizens are constrained or restricted. Where rights constraints are proposed as a way to protect security for a community (especially where they impact some but not all citizens), evaluating the legitimacy of the proposed constraints will require attention to the equality that is central to democratic politics.

What Is Security?

For political theorists, the original consideration of security and its import to individuals is usually traced back to Thomas Hobbes and John Locke. For both Hobbes and Locke, one reason to move from the state of nature to a collectively governed political community is to increase one's individual security. For Hobbes, life in the state of nature is one of perpetual war, whereas for Locke life in the state of nature is generally peaceful. In both cases, individuals are motivated to resolve the insecurities of the state of nature; whereas, for Hobbes, these insecurities are so severe that they prompt individuals to cede nearly all of their rights to the sovereign, for Locke, they are comparatively minor, and so individuals cede only so much authority as is needed to render life in society one in which more freedom can be exercised. Correspondingly, Hobbes believes that the sovereign to whom power

19

is ceded must possess nearly total power in order to preserve security for citizens, whereas Locke believes that the governing authority is ceded only the power needed to ensure that citizens can live in freedom (Meisels 2008).

Political theorists have recently done additional work to define "security." Jeremy Waldron draws on Hobbes' account to note that the core of security lies in *physical* security (Waldron 2003, 2006). Whatever else it means to be secure, it *certainly* means that one is free from physical violence and its threat; this is the "pure safety" account of security. Waldron observes that security also means that one's material possessions are secure – one can leave the house without worrying that it will be burgled – and that there is an expectational dimension to security. A secure individual believes she, and her belongings, are secure presently as well as into the future – i.e., that the conditions that shape her life, and in which she makes choices, are likely to continue into the future.

The sense of one's future security has objective and subjective components. One can be objectively secure or insecure – the likelihood that one will be the victim of a terrorist incident, or that one's home will be burgled, is measurable (Wolfers 1952, 485). However, even where someone is objectively secure, she can *at the same time* believe that she is highly insecure. Where someone is fearful of physical violence, or believes that her way of life is under threat, even where it is objectively not the case, she is insecure in a meaningful way.

In reality, no individual, and no state, can be *perfectly* secure (Baldwin 1997, 15). This means that there is no set of policies that, if adopted, will fully protect a state and its citizens from the dangers of terrorism. Rather, security exists on a continuum. Individuals and states can be more or less secure; and policies can render citizens and states more or less secure. As a result, one challenge in deliberations around whether to adopt a particular "security-protecting" policy is that citizens will disagree about the risks to security they are willing to accept; for some, small risks will render them subjectively insecure, and for others, relatively larger risks can be borne without damaging their sense of security.

Notice the dual usage of the term "security" running through the discussion above. Political actors raising the importance of "national security" seem to be describing a community; Waldron's theorizing, however, describes individuals. In fact, both are apposite: security is properly understood as a feature of communities and of individuals. To return to

21

Waldron's "pure safety" starting point: an individual is secure to the extent that she is physically safe and her subsistence needs are met, presently and (she believes) over time. Similarly, a community is secure to the extent its members are physically safe and generally able to meet their subsistence needs, presently and (they believe) over time.

One might propose that to say that a given community is safe is equivalent to saying its individual members are safe. On this view, the security of the community simply *is* the aggregated security of its individuals. But this does not seem quite right. On the contrary, the observation that "security" can be a feature of communities and of individuals throws into relief the "distributional" questions raised by security. That is, security can be distributed *unequally* in a community (Waldron 2006). Some *neighbourhoods* in a state can be safer than others; some are known for having more drug use or gang violence than others. As well, some individuals in a community can be more secure than others – in most communities, men are still more secure than women, who continue to face higher risks of domestic violence and assault. An overall safe community, in other words, can be composed of citizens, of whom some are safer than others.

Which Rights Matter?

When Ronald Dworkin proposed that rights should be understood as *trumps* against the majority's preferences, he was worried about a situation in which minorities are asked to sacrifice rights in exchange for protecting something of value to the larger community (Dworkin 1981). Dworkin's general worry was that democratic states may sometimes believe that a particular policy, which is preferred by a majority, can legitimately be adopted, *even though* it violates the rights of a minority. Maybe that minority is looked down upon in polite society, or is marginalized in a particular community, and this in part explains why a democratic majority might be willing to violate, or refuse to protect, its rights; when democratic states refused to grant LGBTQ persons the right to marry, for example, the refusal stemmed in part from a discomfort with, and in many cases hatred of, homosexuals. Or maybe – and this is what is at stake in strategies adopted to fight terrorism – the majority believes that the security gain from pursuing particular policies is so significant that a particular minority can be asked, and should be willing, to forsake rights, in the name of collective security for everyone.

In response to this worry, Dworkin proposed

that rights are trumps – i.e., there are certain rights that are so important that they can, in effect, trump the majority's preference. What rights should these be? Usually the answer to which rights should be treated as so important that they should trump majority preferences is the set of rights that are foundational to democratic rule, including rights to due process, to bodily integrity, to freedom of speech, conscience, association, religion and so on (Rawls 1993). A state must protect these rights for all citizens in order to rightfully be described as democratic.

However, in cases of emergency, including terrorist emergencies, many governments believe that even these basic rights can be sacrificed, at least for a very short time period (Lazar 2009). But, whatever the exigencies imposed on governments by terrorist emergencies, there are certain rights that must be protected, and the failure to do so puts the very core of democratic states at risk (Meisels 2008, 78). Tamar Meisels proposes that "certain procedural civil liberties – specifically the right to remain silent under investigation and the related immunity from torture" are rights that cannot be compromised (Meisels 2008, 77). Michael Ignatieff suggests these rights are those that "preclude cruel and unusual punishment, torture, penal servitude, and extrajudicial execution as well as rendition of subjects to rights-abusing countries" (Ignatieff 2004, 24). The objective of delimiting the *basic* rights that are immune from restriction is to press back against those who aim to treat *all* rights as violable in the name of protecting security; so, although there may be disagreement among political theorists around which specific rights count as basic, there is on the contrary considerable agreement that some rights remain sacrosanct even where a state must combat terrorism or other forms of emergency. As a group, these rights "prevent governments from riding roughshod over individuals" (Ignatieff 2004, 5).

Usually, however, democratic states are committed to protecting more than these very basic rights. Democratic states are founded on a commitment to equality, and this is usually understood to protect a wider range of rights than merely the basic ones listed above. Democratic political theorists disagree with respect to how best to understand and protect democratic "equality" (Anderson 1999; White 2007). This book operates with an understanding of equality as equal concern and respect for all members of a democratic state, which in turn translates into a focus on their equal treatment by the state. The needs, interests and preferences of *all* citizens

25

are understood to generate "equally pressing claims on how our society is organized" (White 2007, 11), and correspondingly each citizen's interests count just as much as any other citizen's interests.

There are four major domains in which equal treatment must be protected: civil rights, access to political participation, access to a wider range of social positions and opportunities, and economic benefits. Correspondingly, equal concern and respect requires: (1) the protection of civil rights for all citizens, including freedom of conscience, speech, association and religious expression; (2) the protection of equal access to opportunities to participate in politics, including via access to the vote; (3) the protection of fair terms for competing for valuable social positions, including access to higher education and employment opportunities; and (4) the protection of at least basic economic welfare for all citizens.[1] The precise way in which equality is protected in these domains varies by democratic state, and some states will do more than others to protect more robust forms of equality than others.

---

[1] Many democrats, including this author, believe that much more than this is required, but space constraints prevent a full-throated defense of more robust material equality, and this commitment is not essential to the argument that follows.

This book will not take a position beyond what has so far been articulated, and will simply judge that – so long as the parameters set by a focus on equality as equal concern and respect are met – what matters is that, whatever package of rights is selected by a democratic, political society, it must be protected *equally* for all citizens.

Democratic Equality and Distributing Security

The commitment to equality that underpins democratic states does not mean that there are no moments where it is warranted to treat citizens unequally. It means, rather, that inequalities are permitted only where they are justified (usually in public forums), often with reference to other valuable goods, and that where they are unjustified, good faith efforts are made to remedy them. Correspondingly, proposals by the state that citizens should be treated unequally along some dimension require attention, if not always remedy, from democrats.

There are cases in which unequal treatment should especially worry democrats, however, and this is when it tracks existing social and economic disadvantage (Rawls 1993). In this context, a disadvantage is a feature about an individual, usually a characteristic that is "arbitrary from a moral point of view," that makes it less likely that she achieves success than other, similarly situated, citizens, who do not possess that feature. It is an unfortunate fact that in many democratic states, there are identifiable groups – identified sometimes by race, religion, culture, sexuality, gender and so on – that experience disadvantages of a kind that make it harder for them to access the goods that are supposed to be available to all on an equal basis. Disadvantage can be measured in multiple ways: in terms of the likelihood of being assaulted, of being the victim of discrimination, of being excluded from educational or employment opportunities, of being homeless, of being incarcerated, and so on (Wolff and de-Shalit 2007). When unequal treatment tracks these disadvantages, they are especially worrisome, for at least two reasons: (1) to the extent that inequality is permissible in democratic states, it is permissible only within some boundaries, and compounded disadvantage is most likely to press inequality beyond these boundaries of permissible inequality; and (2) in many (perhaps most) cases of compounded inequalities, their persistence stems in large part from prejudice against those who are subjected to them.

In democratic states, most people who experience disadvantage are not *wholly* socially disadvantaged

– that is to say, many people are subject to disadvantage along some dimensions, but not others. Women may be taken less seriously in STEM professions; certain visible minorities may be more likely to be the victims of assault; obese individuals may be less likely to have their health concerns taken seriously by doctors. In many cases, dimensions of disadvantage converge: women of color may find themselves marginalized from some opportunities because they are women, and from others because they are persons of color, for example. Where members of a particular minority do less well along many of the standards of well-being that are understood to make up a flourishing life in a democratic society, then they are properly described as a disadvantaged minority (Modood 2006).

So, because democracies are in principle committed to equality, unequal treatment should worry democrats in general, as well as to the extent that it tracks or entrenches existing and known disadvantage. As a result, where democracies propose policies that add disadvantage – usually in the form of restricted or constrained rights – to individuals who *already experience* substantial disadvantage, democrats have reason to consider both: (1) if the restriction can be justified by producing some greater good such as security; and also (2) whether, even if a greater good can be obtained, the costs of imposing rights restrictions or constraints is too large to be justified. Note that the suggestion, for now, is simply that *attention* must be given to policies that appear to especially burden minorities who are disadvantaged along multiple dimensions; after consideration of the relevant facts, it may well be judged justified to impose these additional burdens. Chapter 3 considers methods to assess whether this additional burden can be justified.

Security and equality

Equality-respecting democracies face a range of challenges when aiming to protect security by combatting terrorism. Some security-protecting policies have an equal impact on all citizens. The New Zealand policy to ban most semi-automatic firearms, adopted after the mosque shootings, affected all citizens equally.

More often, however, there are security-generating policies that impact citizens differently, in ways that direct attention to the equality considerations that guide policy-making in democratic states. One way that terror prevention policies can challenge a democracy's commitment to equality is by permitting the good of the majority to be a reason to reduce the rights of some, specific, individuals, just as Dworkin worried. Of course, those who commit crimes are *certainly* subject to having their rights restricted as part of their punishment. There is nothing controversial about such restrictions, even if there is important discussion focused on which rights can be justly restricted as part of a fair punishment (see chapter 2). However, many policies that aim at protecting security for all do so by constraining or restricting the freedom of some, specific, individuals *before* a crime has been committed. In some cases, affected individuals may well have been intending harm, and so there may seem to be little reason to be wary of restricting their rights. However, it is inevitable that this type of policy will also implicate some individuals who have no intention of committing a crime, i.e., who are entirely innocent; their rights will also be restricted, and it is right to ask whether this restriction is fair to *them*.

For some, the sacrifice of some individuals' rights to produce security for all might not seem egregiously wrong, when the collective security is believed to be significantly threatened. After all, most rights are subject to trade-offs, both with other rights and with valuable collective goods. Hate speech laws – which limit the kinds of claims individuals can make in public spaces – limit the right to free speech, but this kind of limit is often accepted in democratic states, in order to protect people from those who might otherwise incite hatred or violence, especially against minorities. Environmental protection laws protect the collective health of the community, for example, by requiring car drivers to ensure that their cars meet emissions tests, and, where they do not, by requiring them to repair or upgrade cars so that they do; in so doing, these laws limit the right of individuals to use their own property as they see fit.

These examples illustrate that there are many cases in which individual rights are constrained or restricted to protect a variety of valuable collective goods. However, in cases in which it is proposed that the rights of members of disadvantaged communities are to be restricted, as described earlier, such policies require extra scrutiny, to ensure that they are truly justified and not simply manifestations of prejudice. Consider travel restrictions: passport cancellation laws and no-fly lists deny air travel to suspected foreign fighters, and in so doing restrict their right to movement, in the service of protecting a state's collective security. Yet, at least some evidence suggests that those who are impacted by these policies are disproportionately likely to be citizens with Muslim or Middle Eastern backgrounds (Jamil 2017, 82; Jarvis 2018), who in turn are plausibly described as a disadvantaged minority in many democratic states (Modood 2006). This example will be considered in more detail in chapter 3, where the disparate impact of travel restrictions on Muslim and Muslim-appearing individuals will be weighed against the collective security benefit that they generate.

To conclude this chapter: by definition, terrorism is scary, and its impacts are widely felt, especially in the aftermath of an attack. Part of what makes terrorism scary is that it threatens further, possibly imminent, violence. In the days and weeks following an attack – for example, after September 11 – the number of individuals whose security is threatened is large, and the imperative is to adopt strategies to halt imminent violence (Lazar 2009). In the midst and immediate aftermath of a terrorist emergency, there may be reasons to accept rights restrictions – perhaps even where distributed unequally – to protect collective security (although post-hoc mechanisms to evaluate the actions taken in the midst of an emergency are essential). When the threats of terrorism are more dilute, and attacks are infrequent, states of course maintain their obligation to protect the security of citizens. But, in this case, the collective benefit of any particular counter-terror policy can be nebulous, whereas the costs they impose are certain, and increase in importance as time passes. In particular, rights restrictions that are sometimes attached to imminent, or actualized, threats may not be defensible over the longer term. In the midst of the tentative and nebulous threats that democratic states face on a daily basis, accepting these rights restrictions threatens to undermine other goods that democracies are aimed at producing for their citizens, including especially the trust between citizens, and between citizens and their representatives, that is essential to democratic practice (Lenard 2012).

Going forward, then, it is essential to keep in mind that the provision and protection of security must be attentive to protecting equality; in democratic states, this attention to equality compels sincere discussion of whether some citizens are unfairly subject to rights restrictions, in the name of protecting collective security. Earlier accounts of security have not had enough to say about what kinds of equality are compromised when security is proposed as a reason to subject some individuals to rights restrictions, either as punishment for terrorist crimes or via attempts to prevent it. Chapters 2 and 3 will tackle these questions, respectively, with an attention to protecting the equality that is fundamental to democratic states.

2

Punishing Terrorism in Democratic States

Security matters. One of the state's central jobs is to provide security for its citizens. As the last chapter described, democratic states are obligated not only to provide security, but to provide it in a way that is consistent with democratic egalitarianism. States protect their citizens by preventing crimes (see chapter 3) and by punishing criminals. Democratic states face a particular challenge in determining the appropriate punishment for terrorist crimes – i.e., crimes aimed at generating fear in fellow citizens, often by harming them in public and gruesome ways. Because terrorists aim to instill the kind of fear that renders society unable to produce the set of goods on which its citizens rely, and because living in fear for the future is so "unspeakably awful" (Scheffler 2006, 4), they are often believed to deserve the harshest of possible punishments.

Certainly, this view is widely held among the public, which often endorses the suspension of civil liberties for suspected and convicted terrorists (Newheiser and DeMarco 2018), the torture of suspected terrorists, and the imposition of severe punishment on convicted terrorists.

Yet the determination of just punishments must be done carefully, in a way that is consistent with the principles that underpin an equality-respecting democracy. This determination can seem especially difficult in democratic states that rely on juries to determine guilt: lawyers for Dzhokhar Tsarnaev, the man who bombed the Boston Marathon in 2013, an attack that killed 3 people and injured nearly 300 others, argued that his trial ought to have left Boston because jurors were incapable of seeing through the trauma he inflicted on the city to offer him the fair trial and punishment that he was entitled to as a citizen of the United States (Winter 2018). So, it is clear that determining the just punishment in the case of terrorists is not easy. This chapter describes how an equality-respecting democracy should approach punishing convicted – and, in some cases, merely suspected – terrorists.

The first section of the chapter outlines the many objectives that punishment is said to have, including exacting retribution, supporting rehabilitation and deterring future crime. The second section of the chapter offers an account of the best way to understand the goals of punishment in a democratic state. The commitments that an equality-respecting democracy must hold, outlined in chapter 1, shape the way that punishment's goals should be understood, and correspondingly which kinds are appropriately directed at terrorists. In particular, the chapter suggests, punishment in democratic states must do the following, in order to be consistent with its egalitarian commitments: it must punish following a fair trial, which is conducted in public to the greatest extent possible; it must issue a punishment that, at least in principle, permits the reintegration of the criminal into society with her full set of rights restored; and it must reflect respect for the person who is punished, for the victims of the crimes and for the wider community in which the crime took place.

The second and longer section of the chapter illustrates how this democratic conception of punishment applies in three challenging cases of punishing terrorists. The cases this chapter considers in detail, with a view to illustrating distinct aspects of punishment, are those of Anders Breivik, who murdered 77 Norwegians in 2011, declaring that they deserved it for their abandonment of pure Norwegian values;

Shamima Begum, who left the UK as a 15-year old to join the ISIS caliphate; and Robert Bowers, who targeted and murdered 11 Jews in the United States. The first case highlights the public nature of trials and the corresponding importance of transparency in prosecuting crimes, as well as the merits and demerits of maximum-sentencing laws, which, in Breivik's case, resulted in what many perceived to be a light sentence of 21 years in prison. The second highlights a particularly severe penalty – namely, the revocation of citizenship – which has recently entered the toolkit of available penalties for terrorist crimes in some democratic states, and which is sometimes (as it is in Begum's case) imposed without first attaining a criminal conviction. The third considers "sentencing enhancements" for terrorist crimes, and their logical connection to "hate crime" penalties, which permit states to single out particular crimes for additional penalties because of the perpetrator's intention – specifically, to generate fear among victims.

Punishment in Democratic States

Chapter 1 described the equality that is central to democratic practice in general; this commitment applies to punishment also. Note that a criminal justice system has at least three groups of citizens, with distinct interests, who must be protected and respected. In particular, it must aim to protect the equality of the perpetrator of a crime, the victims of a crime, and the citizens of the society in which the crime was committed (or from which the criminal emerged). These various parties have different relations to the crime and to the punishment exacted, as will be elaborated. Here, it is worth emphasizing that those accused of and punished for crimes are at the mercy of the state – the full apparatus of state power is directed at them, and having been apprehended for possible punishment, they are highly vulnerable to that power. As a result, the justice of a democratic state is on full display when it engages in the complex tasks of apprehending, convicting and punishing criminals.

The public call to exact severe retribution on terrorists highlights the need to take a step back to ask what, morally, is required of democracies as they engage in punishment with a full recognition of the basic rights of all citizens, including perpetrators (Lenard 2019). Below, the chapter will describe three principles of punishment in democratic states, which are appropriate to respecting the three parties with interests in the fairness of a democratic criminal justice system.

First, consider the large body of people who are not directly connected to the crime. Democracies perform much of their business in public, to maintain the confidence of citizens. The principle of transparency is key to democratic political practice, and requires that information about the activities and decisions of policy-makers be relatively accessible to citizens and residents, and thus available for their scrutiny (Fung 2013; Lenard and Macdonald forthcoming). Democracies regularly ask citizens to accept policies and regulations that impose costs on them; and they subject citizens to coercive institutional mechanisms that operate to ensure that these policies and regulations are respected. The willingness of citizens to accept these decisions ideally stems from public deliberations about these policies and regulations, and their attendant costs, in public spaces (Blake 2001).

The importance of transparency in democratic spaces in general applies to the conviction and punishments of crimes, as well. Hidden accusations, trials and punishments are easily abused and strongly associated with authoritarian states. In democratic states, crimes are treated as the violation of the rules and policies of a democracy – which have, ideally, been deliberated and adopted in democratic spaces – and the procedures for applying penalties ought also to take place in public spaces, so that citizens can be confident that the criminal justice system treats victims, and alleged and convicted criminals, fairly.

Before going further, it is worth noting that there is a way in which deploying an *equality* frame to consider how best to shape fair punishment in democratic states may seem confusing in at least one dimension: perhaps, one might think, it is peculiar to focus on the *equality* of both perpetrators and victims. Victims and perpetrators are in highly unequal positions from a moral perspective, in the sense that one has committed a harm against an innocent other. The general claim is a simple one, however: that even perpetrators are members of a community with expectations for treatment that is consistent with, and guided with considerations informed by, equality. In the case of punishment, equality is respected when the basic rights of all individuals are protected; the individual who is punished is, however, made worse off, in the sense that some key rights may be restricted for the duration of her punishment.

A criminal trial is a space in which a prosecutor, acting on behalf of the state, makes the case that an individual has broken the law and correspondingly deserves to be punished. Over the course of the trial, the accused can respond to the claims that she has done wrong. There are many details here which philosophers of punishment deliberate, but a key point is that the trial is, at least in its ideal form, one that is governed by fair terms of engagement that respect the basic rights of all parties and which can be witnessed as such. Some trials, or some aspects of some trials, may be held secretly, where doing otherwise will result in harm, perhaps to the victims or their families. However, the baseline is an open and publicly accessible trial space. In some criminal trials, there may be no specific victim, and in others there may be a range of claimants demanding the application of penalties or recompense of some kind – for example, the victim herself, her family or friends (in case of death), or society at large. The publicity of the trial process is at least in part about ensuring that victims, understood broadly, are appropriately treated and, where relevant, fairly compensated. It is also about providing the information that a political community needs in order to believe that the general legal structure that governs their lives in common is fairly applied.

The importance of treating the victims fairly is not the only concern for equality-respecting democracies; additionally, they have a kind of outer limit to the range of allowable punishments, which stems from the obligations that they have to perpetrators of crimes. It is in the nature of punishment that it *removes* rights from individual wrong-doers, rights that are understood to be among those that are protected for all citizens of a state. So, a punished individual is rendered unfree as a result of her wrongdoing, but since her basic and foundational rights are protected (as they were outlined in chapter 1), her punishment is not typically understood as a violation of her fundamental equality as a citizen.

In order for that to remain true – in order to respect the fundamental equality of those who are subject to punishment in democratic states – it must be the case that the perpetrator can at least in principle return to the community of responsible citizens, with her rights restored, once the punishment is complete (Cohen 2016). On this way of understanding the demands of democratic equality, punishment is "an attempt to engage in forceful moral communication with the offender, it can be a process that addresses the offender as a responsible fellow citizen – and thus be something that citizens could properly do to each other" (Duff 2009, 84).

A supporting observation is that, although the criminal process is subject to very strict rules of engagement, the possibility of convicting and punishing innocents is real; refusing to countenance "permanent" punishments recognizes the fallibility of human judgment, by allowing for redress opportunities for the wrongfully convicted.

Some forms of punishment are thereby ruled out. The commitment to leaving open the possibility that criminals can return to the community as full members, most obviously, rules out capital punishment as a legitimate punishment. Additionally, it means ruling out punishments that extend *beyond* the terms of a prison sentence – this means that the practice of felon disenfranchisement, for example, that extends beyond the serving of a particular sentence, cannot be justified, since it amounts to refusing to allow convicted felons to return to the status of full and equal citizens (Whitt 2017). The same may be true of requiring that convicted criminals, who have carried out their sentences, convey their criminal history to potential employers.

There are more controversial cases that may need to be examined on a case-by-case basis – for example, the practice of denying convicted sex offenders the right to live near schools for children, even after they have carried out their sentence. In other words, there may be situations where the continued restriction of certain rights may, all things considered, be justifiable, even if this impedes the capacity of individuals to regain fully their status as equal members of society. But the lesson here is the same: the way in which rights restrictions that extend beyond the formal duration of a sentence should be evaluated is by asking whether these restrictions deny the capacity of an individual to regain their full and equal status as a citizen.

Finally, in cases where there are victims, democracies must consider the rights of the victim and note the importance of ensuring that the punishment respects her, the victim, in the sense of being in some sense appropriate to the harm done her. In the political theory of punishment, much work focuses on how to measure the harm done, what recompense can be demanded of offenders, and how to know whether that recompense is appropriate or justified. This project is imperfect, since often what is "taken" from a victim cannot in any reasonable way be "taken" from an offender in compensation. Few believe now that the Hammurabi code — an eye for an eye – is what should guide punishment. To take just one example, it is usually agreed that where the crime is rape, it is nevertheless not appropriate – because liberal, democratic states protect the right to bodily integrity – to propose that, as punishment, rapists should be themselves subject to rape. And while even democratic states have historically imposed a range of punishments for violent crimes, from hard labor to chemical castration to death, the most common punishment for serious, violent, crimes is incarceration, accompanied in some cases by financial restitution. So, the main question typically faced by those imposing punishment has to do with how to determine the length of incarceration, so that the punishment is, in some sense, proportionate to the crime. The failure to respect proportionality between the felt gravity of the crime and the punishment meted out is at least in part what has been historically problematic about past attempts to punish sexual assault crimes against women; the harm done to women has been treated historically as relatively insubstantial (or deserved, or understandable), and correspondingly lenient punishments issued to the offenders failed to respect the *equality* of female victims.

In sum, there are three parties to any attempt to punish crimes: the political community at large, the perpetrator and the victims. All three of these parties are entitled to equal treatment over the course of the apprehension, conviction and punishment of crimes, and this commitment to equal treatment – demanded by democratic principle – translates into three general requirements: (1) a publicity requirement, around the apprehension, conviction and punishment of crimes (which respects the equality of the political community); (2) a rehabilitative requirement, according to which perpetrators are in principle able to return to the political community once the punishment has been served (which respects the equality of the perpetrator); (3) a proportionality requirement, which attempts to match the severity of the punishment to the severity of the crime (which respects the equality of the victim). In the section that follows, three case studies will do more to emphasize and highlight how these three equality principles are deployed (or ought to be deployed) in the cases of suspected and actual terrorists.

Just Punishments in Democratic States

In 2011, in Norway, Anders Breivik detonated a van bomb, killing 8 people, and went on to shoot and kill another 69. Those he shot were participating in a summer camp associated with the Workers' Youth League, a political organization for young people affiliated with the Norwegian Labor Party; Breivik explained that he was intending to punish members of this party for their contribution to the takeover of Norway by Muslims. In advance of his attack, he wrote a manifesto in which he argued for the deportation of all Muslims and the importance of protecting Nordic purity from them. Although he did not attack Muslim citizens and residents of Norway directly in his attack, his clear objective was to send a message to them, and those who support them, that they are unwelcome. Breivik was charged with and convicted of committing terrorist acts, aimed at instilling fear in the Norwegian population and undermining its institutions (*BBC News* 2012).

Breivik was sentenced to 21 years in prison for his horrific, *terrorist*, crimes, the maximum that Norwegian law permits. The option to impose additional preventative detention was made available, 5 years at a time, if the appropriate authorities believe that, after 21 years, he persists in being a threat to Norwegian society. For many non-Norwegians, the punishment appeared inadequate to the crimes he had committed. The opening line of a commentary in the *Atlantic* magazine reads, "As an American, or maybe just as a moral human being, it's hard not to feel appalled, even outraged, that Norwegian far-right monster Anders Breivik only received twenty-one years in prison" (Fisher 2012). This outrage reflects both the horror that observers felt in response to the crime itself, and the discomfort that many felt with respect to the extensive public platform Norway gave over the course of the trial to Breivik to express his hateful views. The trial was designed not only to assess what sort of punishment was appropriate (his guilt was never in doubt), but also to allow him to speak his mind in his own defense. At no point during the trial did Breivik express remorse for his actions; rather, he used the public space to defend their contribution to rendering Norway free of its many threats.

Nevertheless, many Norwegians defended the apparently "light" maximum sentence available. Said one survivor of the shootings, "If he is deemed not to be dangerous any more after 21 years, then he should be released ... That's how it should work. That's staying true to our principles and the best evidence that he hasn't changed our society" (Lewis and Lyall 2012). Regarding the trial, many observers worried that giving Breivik a platform to express his views would serve only to inspire further attacks. Yet silencing him, they also believed, would have undermined the benefits of an open and transparent trial, denying Norwegians the opportunity to observe and deliberate whether justice was being done.

Consider, now, the case of Shamima Begum. In 2015, she left the United Kingdom to join ISIS as a so-called "jihadi bride." She is said to have contributed to ISIS efforts by enforcing its morality on others and by encouraging other young women to join its ranks; some sources additionally allege she was responsible for sewing suicide vests on in such a way that they could not be removed without detonating (Hall and Dearden 2019). During the time she spent in ISIS territory, she gave birth to at least two children, both of whom died from illness or malnutrition. In early 2019, she turned up at a refugee camp in Syria, heavily pregnant, asking to return to the UK.

In response to her request, the UK government moved to rescind her citizenship, the practical effect of which has been to deny her ability to return to the UK as she has requested. As part of this move to rescind her citizenship, the UK government has alleged she has ongoing access to Bangladeshi citizenship – a claim that she and the government of Bangladesh both deny. Though her parents are Bangladeshi in origin, Begum was born, and grew up, in the United Kingdom; she has never visited Bangladesh, nor does she speak its language. The law permitting the revocation of Begum's citizenship allows the move when it is believed that an individual has behaved, or is likely to behave, "in a manner which is seriously prejudicial to the vital interests of the UK" – although typically only so long as it is believed that the individual has reasonable access to citizenship elsewhere (Gibney 2013). Whether these conditions are met in the Begum case is not clear, and legal proceedings are ongoing, with Begum's family's lawyers disputing both that she is entitled to Bangladeshi citizenship and that revocation is thereby permissible. Defending Begum's denationalization, a UK Home Office spokesperson said "In recent days, the Home Secretary has clearly stated that his priority is the safety and security of Britain and the people who live here. In order to protect this country, he has the power to deprive someone of their British citizenship where it would not render them stateless" (Rawlinson and Dodd 2019).

The banishment of citizens has a long pedigree, starting at least with the Ancient Athenians, who "ostracized" citizens – which meant banishment from the city-state for 10 years – who were believed to threaten Athenian democracy (Forsdyke 2009). After this time, they were permitted to return to Athens, with their rights intact, and to the property they had left behind, but ideally with diminished political power. The practice of exile persisted through centuries, often deployed as a punishment that was understood by both perpetrator and the state as *less* severe than alternatives, including state-sanctioned torture or execution (Kingston 2005). In the aftermath of World War II, however, the international legal order recognized the importance of citizenship status (Arendt 1963), and multiple conventions following World War II acknowledged the importance of the right to citizenship, codified in Article 15 of the Universal Declaration of Human Rights as the "right to nationality." Article 15 also requires that states refrain from withdrawing it "arbitrarily."

The post-World War II era saw a corresponding decline in the use of revocation laws in democratic states – many of which, however, remain on the books (Groot and Vink 2010). Across several states, including in the UK, Denmark, Norway and Australia, these have recently been adopted or revived as states develop and expand their terrorism-fighting toolkit (Thwaites 2016). The revocation of citizenship is one way, its defenders argue, that states can appropriately punish those who engage in terrorist activities: along with capital punishment, it is the only punishment that, to many, appears appropriately severe.

Can the UK justifiably revoke Begum's citizenship, then, as a *punishment* for her alleged crimes? Notice, first, that expulsion as a punishment fails to meet the requirements of an appropriate and fair punishment in democratic states (Macklin 2014; Lenard 2016, 2018). It is *permanent*, even in the case of dual nationals. It treats individuals who perpetrate certain crimes as having carried out an action that is so egregious that they cannot return to the state as full and equal citizens.

But, one might respond, the crime that Begum is accused of is no ordinary crime. By joining ISIS, an existential enemy of the United Kingdom, she declared herself to be a threat to the UK. Furthermore, her actions demonstrate a willingness to forsake the protection of UK laws, so, in effect, by her *actions*, she has self-revoked her citizenship. The UK is acting only to legalize a choice that she herself made, the objection concludes.

This view is in part buttressed by ideas generated from social contract theories of the state. On these views, the state and citizens should be understood as having signed a contract, in which each has duties to carry out. The state's duties include protecting citizens from harm; the citizens' duties include doing their part to sustain the democratic institutions that govern them. For those who characterize the state–citizen relationship in this way, it is appropriate to expel citizens who, instead, act to undermine the democratic institutions that govern them – for example, by choosing to side with organizations that aim at undermining these same democratic institutions. Since they have failed to carry out their duties as part of the contract, correspondingly the state is released from its duty to offer them protection. It is therefore appropriate and proportionate to the crime to expel those who aim, by their actions, to undermine a state's capacity to function (Joppke 2016). So, on this view, Begum's citizenship can be revoked, and she can justifiably be denied the right to return to the UK (for an overview of arguments defending and rejecting revocation, see Ferracioli 2017).

This reasoning should be rejected for two reasons, however. One reason is the genuine challenge of interpreting *intention* from someone's behaviors. In the US Supreme Court case that rendered revocation of citizenship unconstitutional, at issue was whether a US (naturalized) citizen who had voted in an Israeli election intended to revoke his citizenship by doing so. The Court determined that it was near impossible to be certain what someone *intended* by their actions, and the result was that revocation of citizenship was deemed permissible only when explicit and voluntary (Weil 2012). In Begum's case, some media reported that she maintained the conviction that her choice to join ISIS was a good one, and they focused on her alleged lack of remorse for the crimes she committed. More recent reporting has suggested that her lack of expressed remorse stemmed from an ongoing fear of being harmed by ISIS as she remains in a territory with many ISIS sympathizers (Drury 2019). If she has expressed ongoing support for ISIS under duress, then her intention to rejoin the UK, and face punishment there for her crimes, should not be rejected. Moreover, even if it were the case that Begum had wanted to reject the UK state at one point, she may well no longer desire that; if her desires have changed, a punishment that is justified only or mainly on the basis of past desires may be unreasonable. The point here is that her intentions in the past, and going forward, are deeply unclear, and this means that her actions ought not to be taken to mean that she has disavowed her UK citizenship permanently.

Second, Begum has not yet had access to a criminal trial, in which the state lays out its case against her and in which she can explain, and defend, her actions. A full airing of those facts could even help to calm the chorus of voices calling for her expulsion from the British state. States are sometimes reluctant to accuse alleged terrorists in court because they worry about their capacity to meet evidentiary requirements where crimes have been committed abroad. This worry may be real, but it ought not to translate into a violation of the obligation to prosecute crimes in a public space, in which the accused can mount a defense. So Begum's punishment should give pause even to those who support the revocation of citizenship for terrorist criminals, because she has so far been denied the right to defend herself.

The purpose of considering these two cases together is to highlight two profoundly different strategies that states can take when they punish suspected and convicted terrorists. In the Norwegian case, the punishment procedure takes seriously that all individuals should be treated as capable of being full, equal, rights-bearing members of a democratic society. In principle, Breivik can be integrated into Norwegian society once he has served his sentence, under the condition that he understands and takes responsibility for the crimes he has committed (presently, no evidence suggests that he has absorbed the gravity of his crimes). Yet Begum, should her citizenship remain revoked, will be denied access to full and equal membership in British society, even were she to come to absorb the gravity of her criminal acts; she will remain banished from British society, left to struggle as an effectively stateless person to protect her rights in a refugee camp in former ISIS territory, to which she fled as a child. She would thereby be denied an opportunity to defend herself in a public space, as well as the opportunity to return to a society of equals.

Some readers might concede that, in the case of single-nationality citizens, rendering someone stateless as a form of punishment is so severe as to count as cruel and unusual, and is therefore morally unavailable to democratic states. Indeed, even among democratic states that permit revocation for terrorist acts, it is typically permitted only on the condition that the convicted terrorist would not thereby be rendered stateless. The additional *democratic* reason for rejecting revocation in this sort of case is that it denies an individual access to important democratic political rights. If this is one's view, one might permit revocation in the case of dual nationals (as Begum is alleged to be) convicted of terrorist crimes who, were they to be denationalized, would retain citizenship and correspondingly political access to another country.

But revocation is problematic even in these cases. Recall that, in democratic states, the baseline principle is that all citizens are entitled to equal treatment. This commitment is violated when two individuals are convicted of the same crime, but one is punished more harshly than the other. Studies demonstrating, for example, that black Americans are sentenced more harshly than white Americans for similar crimes are ample (e.g., Rehavi and Starr 2014); these disparities are widely believed to be violations of the equal treatment to which black Americans are entitled. Notice, then, that revocation in the case of dual citizens permits two people, convicted of the same crime, to be punished differently, simply on the basis of one's nationality. This difference is, on its face, a violation of democratic equality; indeed, many democratic constitutions, including both the Canadian and the American constitutions, explicitly prohibit discrimination against naturalized citizens, who make up a significant portion of dual nationals.

So, revocation of citizenship is a violation of democratic equality. Does this mean that all enhanced punishments are violations of democratic equality? Consider two cases of enhanced punishments: terrorist sentencing enhancements and hate crime enhancements. Terrorist enhancements are additional penalties attached to crimes that are believed to have been committed as a form of terrorism or in support of terrorism (Said 2014).[1] Similarly, hate crime penalties are enhanced penalties applied to criminals whose crimes appear to be motivated

---

[1] Note that the question of sentencing enhancement is separate from recent legislative moves to make new categories of terrorist crimes – for example, offering material support to organizations that are designated "terrorist" (Wattad 2006). These new crimes typically are designed to permit punishment of actions that were not previously treated as criminal.

by hate against a so-called "protected class" of persons. Protected classes are typically groups of individuals who have historically suffered, or are presently suffering, disadvantage on the basis of their membership in that group – for example, due to race, ethnicity, gender and sexuality. The additional "protection" offered by this status is one way that states signal their commitment to protecting the right to equal treatment possessed by disadvantaged communities. In both cases, just as sentencing judges are, in general, permitted to consider a range of contextual factors when imposing particular sentences, they may, this book suggests just below, consider the existence of a terrorist or hate motive.

Recall that one defining feature of terrorist activities is the intention to render a population fearful and, in so doing, undermine the felt security of citizens; correspondingly, counter-terrorism measures are aimed in part at protecting actual and felt security of citizens. Just as terrorist crimes intend to create general fear in a population, hate crimes intend to create fear, usually, in all members of the group who share an identity with those who were targeted by a crime. So the logic of enhanced punishments is the same in both cases: the intention to generate profound, even existential, fear over and above the commission of a heinous crime, can warrant enhanced punishments.[2]

Why defend the right of democratic states to impose enhanced punishments on terrorists, who intend to sow fear, but stop short of permitting revocation of citizenship or capital punishment? The answer is again that punishments must be attentive to the importance of treating three parties fairly: the victim, the criminal, and the wider community in which the crime took place. So, while the enhancements are justified with respect to the victim (hate crime penalties) and the wider community (terrorist enhancements and hate crime penalties), some punishments are ruled out nevertheless from a commitment to the equality of the perpetrator.

A commitment to the perpetrator's equality imposes at least two constraints on proposed enhanced punishments. One is that they must be restricted to cases where a community interest is demonstrably at stake. One challenge with this justification for enhanced punishments is, as it was in the case of revocation above, that it is nearly impossible to know *certainly* what the motive for certain crimes is. The danger in inferring

[2] Although this argument cannot be made here, this parallel is one reason to consider that many hate crimes in fact qualify as domestic terrorism.

motives (i.e., to generate fear) from action, perhaps wrongly, and then on the basis of these putative motives imposing harsher punishments, including revocation, is high (Taylor 2018, 103–4): it presses democratic states dangerously close to permitting the arbitrary application of punishment. Enhanced punishments are thereby justified only where there is clear evidence of the intent to create fear, and where the community's well-being is transparently at stake. A second constraint is, to repeat, that some punishments – including the death penalty and the revocation of citizenship – are impermissible because they permanently exclude perpetrators from the democratic community, denying the possibility of rehabilitation and return to the community. To return to Begum's case, the result of the analysis above is that, supposing she had access to a fair trial and was convicted of terrorism, she would justifiably be liable to enhanced punishment, but not to denationalization.

By way of concluding this chapter, consider the decision to add "hate crime" to the list of crimes Robert Bowers is accused of committing, when he entered a synagogue in Pittsburgh in October 2018 and murdered 11 Jews. Before his attack, he had posted anti-Semitic commentary online, targeting in particular the Hebrew Immigrant Aid

Society (HIAS), which offers support to refugees and asylum seekers in the United States. The synagogue he entered was reported to be a strong supporter of HIAS. According to at least one of the formal complaints issued against him, Bowers declared that he wanted all Jews to die, because, he believed, they were committing genocide against his people (Chavez, Grinberg and McLaughlin 2018). He has been charged with multiple hate crimes for his actions, and, if convicted of these, additional penalties will be issued on top of the sentence for (mere) murder of others.

Additional penalties can be imposed on Bowers, justifiably, because his objective was to instill fear in a vulnerable minority, entitled to protection. In practice, even without the additional "hate crime" charges, Bowers' crimes already carry a maximum sentence of life without parole; so, the practical effect of these additions is minimal. Yet, in this case, the symbolic effect of recognizing Bowers' intent to terrorize Jews is one way in which authorities can acknowledge their entitlement to live in a community without fear. Bowers' crime – and others like his – is not simply murder, but rather murder as a vehicle to render others who share identity markers with those he targeted fearful for their lives. As in the case of Begum, he may not legitimately be *exiled* from a state. Bowers' entitlement to equal treatment requires that his rehabilitation must be considered possible, and his victims' entitlement to equal treatment allows that his punishment may be more severe than a "mere" murderer's.

Conclusion

This chapter began by positing that equality considerations are a key part of the fair punishment of individuals in democratic states, even where criminals aim at threatening the security of citizens. Punishment has multiple objectives, and this chapter has proposed that the right way to understand it is in terms of protecting the actual and felt security of citizens in a democratic state, in part via a commitment to respecting the equality of perpetrators, victims and the wider community. Then the chapter proceeded by detailing the punishments meted out, or available for, three terrorists, whose crimes are distinct in many ways, and whose punishment is being deliberated in distinct ways. The point of the chapter ultimately has been to signal that, even where crimes are grievous, attention must be given to the appropriate treatment of perpetrators, as well as victims and society at large. In some cases, this permits *enhanced* punishment, the chapter proposed, but never the permanent exile of individuals from the community.

3

Preventing Terrorism

Punishment is one way that states combat crime, including terrorism. The threat of punishment also serves, at least in part, to deter terrorist actions – perhaps, say some, if the punishments for crimes are sufficiently harsh they will deter people from wrongdoing. However, the threat of punishment by itself fails to deter would-be criminals fully (e.g., Nagin 2013). So states engage in additional strategies to prevent individuals from engaging in terrorism, and they take myriad forms, including the preventative detention of terrorist suspects; the restriction of speech to limit opportunities for incitement to terrorism; the surveillance of individuals and communities physically and online; the use of no-fly policies to deny or reduce travel opportunities for suspected terrorists, and so on.

All of these policies impose costs on those who

are subject to them – some of whom are guilty and some of whom are innocent – usually in the form of restricted or constrained rights. This chapter begins by articulating a framework for evaluating when democratic states should prioritize security over the rights of individuals suspected of intending to commit terrorist acts, in the knowledge that many such suspects will in fact be innocent. A "security test" will provide useful questions for proposed or existing counter-terrorism policies, to weigh whether they are acceptable to democratic states. To illustrate how the security test can be used to think through the merits of specific terrorism-prevention policies, this chapter will focus on three cases: expansion of speech prohibitions; restrictions on freedom of movement of suspected foreign fighters; and the surveillance of individuals and communities at risk of radicalization. In the latter two cases, only some individuals are targeted by the terrorism-prevention policy, and so the chapter assesses the mechanisms by which targets are selected. The chapter concludes that there will be occasions when democracies must worry about the ways in which preventing terrorism is being carried out, especially because it often – implicitly or explicitly – profiles potential wrongdoers using illegitimate criteria, including, particularly, racial criteria. The result is to create suspicion of, and distrust among, members of minorities who are often already victims of substantial disadvantage, as described in chapter 1. In some of these cases, it may be reasonable to abandon or modify a prevention policy, to prioritize the protection of citizens' equal access to rights or to reduce the costs imposed on minority citizens, rather than pursue marginal gains in collective security. The overarching worry, explored in the book's conclusion, is that unjustified costs imposed on minority citizens threaten to reduce their willingness to cooperate with counter-terror policies that would, otherwise, render all citizens more secure.

A Security Test

Three straightforward considerations are offered to evaluate policies that are proposed for their contribution to protecting security: whether a proposed policy targets grave and plausible security threats; whether the costs it imposes are proportional to the likely benefits it generates; and whether its operation is sufficiently transparent (Lenard and Macdonald forthcoming). Together, these three considerations form what below is referred to as the "security test."

The first consideration asks whether the proposed policy is aimed at protecting a state's *basic* security (Shue 1996). As chapter 1 suggested, security is a key ingredient of any political society, including democratic ones. In particular, it is a necessary condition for democratic practice; thus, to the extent that a particular policy proposes to protect this security, and to the extent that without this particular policy this basic security is threatened, it may be warranted. As a result, any policy proposed in the name of protecting "security" must be targeting the protection of major political, institutional infrastructure in some way. This is in part an evidentiary question that requires considering whether there is a security threat, and how grave or likely it is. On the one hand, when US President Trump offered national security as a reason to justify the imposition of tariffs on imported steel, for example, or when his administration cited national security as a reason to justify broad roundups of irregular migrants, it was not clear that what was at stake was in fact *security* of this basic type. Threats that target the functioning of democratic institutions, on the other hand, threaten security in this basic sense.

The second consideration asks whether the likely

impact of a proposed policy on those who are targeted by it is proportionate to the threat faced – that is to say, it considers the freedoms that individual people may be asked to sacrifice, or the other costs they may be required to bear, in order to achieve collective security. To meet this standard, a policy that imposes costs on citizens must be defended as the least harmful way to achieve a particular goal. Moreover, where a proposed policy imposes costs on only some members, those who bear the unequal costs are entitled not only to an explanation of why this is the best way to achieve an objective, but also to assurance that other, less costly, policies cannot achieve the objective in question.

Another way of thinking about this particular consideration is with reference to John Rawls' principle of legitimacy for liberal, democratic states. As Rawls explains, the exercise of political power is legitimate where *all* citizens can reasonably be expected to "endorse" it – that is, to recognize the plausibility of the reasons that justify its use, as well as the goal at which it aims (Rawls 1993, 137). Any explanation for unequal cost imposition, then, can only be acceptable where no options are better able to achieve a particular objective, and the objective to be achieved is one that is of value to all members of a community. One additional reason to be attentive to the costs of particular policies is that many who bear them will be *innocent*, and these cost bearers in particular may be prevented from engaging in an activity that they have every right to engage in.

The third consideration is that the adoption and operation of a particular policy must be carried out transparently. This requirement is similar to the value of open trials in ensuring that the application of punishment is consistent with democratic principles, and stems from the same understanding of the role of transparency in democratic processes more generally. Where government actors make choices that are transparent to constituents, constituents can in turn evaluate these choices and hold the actors accountable for them. Here is the Canadian "National Security Transparency Commitment" acknowledging this reality: "Canadians have a responsibility to hold their Government to account for its decisions. This is essential to our democracy. To do so, citizens must know *what* the Government does to protect national security, *how* the Government does it, and *why* such work is important" (Government of Canada 2017).

As with proportionality, transparency is particularly important in cases where proposed policies impose burdens on some but not others. The reasons for choosing policies that impose burdens unequally must be made available for public scrutiny – it is the only way to mitigate the worry that the game is fixed against those who are asked to bear their costs.

An objection might be launched at the transparency requirement in the case of security policies: it may be thought that certain security policies are effective only if they are kept secret. Policies such as surveillance, undercover infiltration, profiling and cyber attacks depend on their being able to operate without the knowledge of their targets. The requirement of transparency remains a requirement even where this may be the case, however.

First, there will be cases where it is appropriate to discuss policies in general, while keeping the operation of the policy somewhat secret. For example, it is possible to deliberate publicly about whether police officers should be permitted to place GPS trackers on cars without warrants, without requiring them to identify which specific cars they are tracking. Second, there is a vast array of institutional options available, between the extremes of something like full ministerial discretion over the adoption of security-protection policies, which in the vast majority of cases will not meet the test outlined here, and fully open public discussion of these same policies, which will do. One can imagine constructing tribunals, or court-like systems, that allow some transparency to be achieved in cases where full, democratic, transparency would compromise the effectiveness of a security policy (Lenard and Macdonald forthcoming). The point is simply that institutional mechanisms that protect transparency are essential to meeting the transparency dimension of the security test.

In sum, the security test is meant to be diagnostic – it is offered as a way to work through whether security-protecting policies can be justified, where they impose rights restrictions or constraints, or other costs, on citizens. Does this mean that a policy that fails the test should be abandoned immediately? Not necessarily, especially if evidence can be adduced that it offers a real benefit to collective security. In these cases, the security test may highlight what must be done to ensure that a particular policy is consistent with democratic principle, by directing policy-makers to focus more on proportionality or transparency requirements.

The rest of this chapter centers on applying the test to three major categories of counter-terror policies: the expansion of speech prohibitions, the restriction of travel, and the surveillance of communities. In each case, a benefit to collective security is posited, and judged plausible, and this benefit is said to justify the imposition of a variety of burdens on citizens and residents, mainly in the form of constrained or restricted rights. The first case differs in form from the latter two; in principle, changes to speech laws impact everyone, whereas travel restrictions and surveillance policies require *selecting* targets. So, a discussion of fair selection strategies precedes the application of the security test to the latter two policies.

The Right to Free Speech and Prohibiting Extremist Speech

To persist over time, terrorist groups must recruit others to their cause. Much recruitment of potential terrorists now happens online, where there are multiple spaces in which individuals filled with hate or frustration can share their views, and where recruiters operate to draw individuals into terrorist networks. These spaces are attractive to those who harbor hatred, as well as to those who desire to recruit and mobilize terrorist actors, since they allow for efficient and relatively anonymous communication and coordination. The worry that these spaces are breeding grounds for the spread of terrorism has generated multiple distinct attempts to limit them.

One terrorist-prevention strategy expands the category of speech that is criminalized, by, in particular, expanding the set of statements that count as incitement to terrorist violence. This proposed enlargement of the category of criminalized speech is part of a general attempt to reduce the capacity of terrorists to communicate and coordinate online. One variation on this strategy is reflected in the British 2006 Terrorism Act, which rendered illegal "statements which are likely to be understood as a direct or indirect encouragement or other inducement to the commission of terrorist acts" (Barendt 2009, 445). The Act additionally clarified that glorification of terrorist actions under some conditions would also constitute an offense, including where, as result of an utterance, "members of the public would reasonably infer that they should emulate them" (Barendt 2009, 445).

The security test applied to online terrorist–extremist speech

In applying the security test, the first question to consider is whether the proposed policy is genuinely aimed at protecting the basic security that underpins the proper functioning of democratic states. Online spaces – including platforms such as Instagram, Facebook, Twitter and YouTube, or web-based online communities, such as Gab, Reddit and 8kun – permit their users to share their hatreds, seek converts and encourage violence. In some cases, these spaces are frequented by recruiters whose objective is to create a global movement of "soldiers" committed to undermining democratic state institutions by generating fear and anxiety among their populations. In others, they serve as a kind of echo chamber, in which hateful ideas are circulated and legitimated by others; democratic states, especially diverse ones, have a strong interest in ensuring that these ideas do not gain currency.

Although very few of those who participate – even actively – in these online spaces radicalize in ways that propel them to conduct acts of terror, there is some suggestion that, among those who do conduct these acts, participation in such spaces has played a role in their formation as terrorists (von Behr et al. 2013). Of course, the evidence here is in its infancy, and this is important. There is certainly evidence that many of the most high-profile far-right extremist murderers are highly sophisticated social media users, as are recruiters to the violent extremist causes (Hankes et al. 2019). What is still being investigated is whether, and how, internet spaces in which far-right extremists and violent religious extremists communicate radicalize individuals to the extent that they transform into terrorists; perhaps, it is argued, already radicalized individuals frequent these sites. It may be wrong, in other words, to conclude from the fact that so many high-profile terrorists have active online lives that all people with such lives are at risk of terrorizing others. It will remain important to be attentive to the evidence as it is gathered; for now, however, so long as the evidence continues to demonstrate that these spaces persist as active forums in which hateful ideas are freely exchanged and legitimated, and in which recruiting and radicalization transpire, it is reasonable to agree that the collective security of a state is threatened by their unregulated presence.

The second security-test question considers whether policies that expand the set of restricted speech acts are proportionally appropriate, in an effort to curb radicalization that can lead to terrorism. What specifically is the harm done by expanding restricted speech? The cost is to the right to freedom of speech, which democracies typically treat as a fundamental, basic, right; John Stuart Mill famously defended it as the key component to living a free and flourishing life (Mill 1991). Additionally, the ability to speak freely is central to the deliberation that is key to policy-making in democratic spaces, and autonomous democratic actors are entitled to hear a wide range of views with respect to particular policy choices. The protection of the right to criticize one's government is treated as especially important in democratic states; citizens must be permitted to mobilize and mount oppositional politics, and, to do so, freedom of speech – even speech that the state does not like – has to be protected.

There are limits to freedom of speech, of course – including, especially, incitement to violence: in many democratic states, using speech to encourage others to engage in criminal activity, especially violent criminal activity, has been criminalized as a justified limit on speech. However, defining "incitement to violence" is a difficult exercise, and Mill's lesson is that attempts to identify the parameters of speech that is prohibited because it incites violence must be conducted carefully, with a bias toward the protection of speech. It will be hard to distinguish between incitement to violence, which should not be protected by freedom of speech, and other forms of encouragement and indoctrination; the line between them may well be "more difficult to draw in the context of terrorist activities," especially when so much of this happens online (Gelber 2019), and when the object of "incitement" is not specified. For example, ISIS invites its "soldiers" to undertake attacks on infidels, but this invitation is not directed at any soldier in particular. Those who *receive* this speech may be citizens, certainly, and it may be wise to adopt non-criminal strategies for engaging with those who do (imagine, for example, informing parents if children are known to frequent certain "terrorist" websites). Yet the speech that is targeted by those who would ban some forms of terrorist speech is often focused on instilling fear – in general among a population, and sometimes among particular minority groups – and for this reason the proposition that it be banned may be worth consideration. Moreover, the harm of being denied the right to utter "terrorist–extremist speech" may be small – even if what counts as incitement is broadened to include encouragement – given the wide scope that would in principle remain for voicing opposition to a particular state's policies.

There is an additional consideration, as well, which is that there is evidence that some speech is *sticky*, i.e., some speech, once heard – even if patently false and repudiated vociferously in public spaces – can render certain ideas plausible and attractive to some listeners (Lepoutre 2019). In particular, when a hateful view is expressed in public, its denunciation requires repeating that view and then explaining its falsity – but the danger exists that the repetition of the view, even to refute it, gives some currency to the view itself. There is some evidence that hateful views, such as the ones expressed in far-right extremist forums, are particularly robust against counter-speech (cited in Lepoutre 2019, notes 20–3); so Mill's proposal that harmful views be aired, so they can be countered, may not always serve the best interests of democratic states. This evidence lends some support to the suggestion that the costs, to freedom of speech, of expanding the domain of prohibited speech can be justified.

The third security-test question is whether expanding the domain of prohibited speech meets the transparency requirement. One challenge launched against Britain's 2006 Terrorism Act highlighted the vagueness of the definition of newly proscribed speech; multiple critics suggested the text of the Act did not clearly delineate what sort of speech was thereby prohibited (Choudhury 2009, 467–73). The dangers posed by vagueness in defining newly prohibited speech are many: state overreach in prosecuting offenders, for example, and the worry that the discretion that informs whom to prosecute is arbitrary. As one scholar notes, "to extend the scope of the criminal law by proscribing speech encouraging terrorism is dangerous, because it enables the government to prosecute extreme political speech it dislikes, perhaps for very good reason, while not intervening in other circumstances where it is more sympathetic to the speech" (Barendt 2009, 453). Particular cases may be at the boundary between acceptable and unacceptable, and these should be open for debate; yet, if one cannot be sure in general terms which speech acts are banned, then the law is not adequately transparent.

In sum, what does the security test tell us about expanding the domain of prohibited speech? It tells us that the reasons to consider criminalizing speech that contains certain forms of encouragement of terrorism in ways that fall short of current legal definitions of incitement are, at least, plausible; the intent of this speech is to generate fear, and this intent, compounded by the danger posed by its stickiness, makes it a plausible threat to a state's basic security. It cautions, however, that the content of banned speech must be made clear and that the decision to constrain must be evidence-based. Efforts to decipher which sorts of speech are dangerous and therefore constrainable will remain a challenge, even if in principle justifiable, and the transparency requirement demands that deliberations around these questions, including the (security-related) evidence in favor of restrictions of certain forms of speech, are made publicly available. This latter requirement entails public debate around whether constraints on speech capture too much, thereby constraining the right to freedom of speech in problematic ways.

Selecting the Targets of Prevention Policies

Where the domain of prohibited speech expands, everyone is affected; there are claims that *everyone* is denied the right to make. Many security policies are just like this, i.e., they apply to all citizens and residents, as did New Zealand's newly adopted ban on most semi-automatic firearms, as mentioned in Chapter 1. Others apply equally to all individuals who are engaging in a particular task; speed cameras on the top of traffic lights monitor all drivers, and employers sometimes monitor the internet activity of all employees. In others, such as the bulk screening of emails for targeted key words, the policy effects everyone uniformly at least in principle – though there are, of course, questions about which words are the subject of searches. In the case of many other security policies, however, security authorities are involved in making choices about whom in particular to target, for example for placement on a no-fly list, or about which neighborhoods to monitor via CCTV (if not all of them). Sometimes, security authorities are seeking a particular individual whom they have reason to believe is likely to harm others; in these cases, highly targeted surveillance techniques, such as wiretapping, are permitted, though generally only with a judge's authorization for a particular target, for which individualized evidence must be produced. Between prevention policies that target specific individuals and those that target everyone in a jurisdiction, there are policies that target certain groups of individuals for prevention policies, usually on the basis of a set of shared characteristics (Hadjimatheou 2014).

The next two terrorism-prevention policies demand not only that the security test evaluates the policy for its contribution to collective security, but also that the *selection* mechanism for its targets is scrutinized. The selection mechanism requires scrutiny both for transparency and for proportionality. There are costs associated with being targeted by any counter-terrorism policy; in cases where only some citizens are targeted for the constraints and restrictions they impose, there are extra costs for those who are selected as targets. In particular, being targeted can have *stigmatizing* effects, from two perspectives. One perspective is that of the individual who is targeted. Especially if she is innocent, she may experience the targeted rights constraint or restriction as humiliating, since being a selected target suggests that she is (to her mind unjustly) believed to be dangerous or suspicious (Hadjimatheou 2014, 189). It is worth again recalling here that many – indeed most – of those whose rights are constrained via counter-terror policies will be innocent. Being targeted may also be stigmatizing from a community perspective. This worry is especially salient when identifiable groups of individuals, who share religious or racial traits, are believed to be selected for special attention. This is, of course, the danger of *racial profiling*, which can serve to "exacerbate existing prejudices against them [i.e., those who are targeted] or even create new ones" (Hadjimatheou 2014, 190).

Note that profiling is not itself *necessarily* problematic. To profile, usually, just means to identify characteristics of a person or group of people that singles them out for some relevant reason: companies construct profiles of their customers, for example, so that their products can be targeted to their needs, or so that they can better identify who is likely to be interested in purchasing their products. Doctors have profiles of patients who are more likely to be susceptible to certain ailments, with whom they engage in more targeted types of care. Nothing is objectionable about this kind of profiling: its objective is, broadly, the efficient delivery of goods to those who are predicted to need them most. Profiling of this type will not always be 100 percent effective: companies can be wrong about who might make best use of their products, and doctors can ignore patients who suffer from an ailment but who are not in the profile they were targeting. But in very general terms, it is normal and reasonable that many service providers target their services and interventions to those who "fit the profile" of those who can best enjoy, or make use of, them.

Police, and other security providers, also engage in profiling. In the case of counter-terror measures, the choice to focus very narrowly on individuals who are known to be in close contact with extremists allows security authorities to target their efforts; but, sometimes, security authorities cast a wider net, based on criteria that they believe can isolate a group of individuals who are more likely to be engaged in wrongdoing of various kinds. This type of targeting can make sense for security authorities, for the same reason that it does when doctors or companies engage in it: providing security is an expensive endeavor, and it is more efficient if they can direct their limited resources toward those who are most likely to commit certain crimes. In some of these cases, it may be that the profile of individuals engaged in wrongdoing includes many markers, including racial ones; as a result, there may be cases where racial profiling serves to aid security agents to most efficiently provide a highly valued good – namely security (Risse and Zeckhauser 2004).

Racial profiling is highly controversial, however. It picks out characteristics of an individual that are supposed to be morally arbitrary (Rawls 1993), and appears to make them relevant in a morally problematic way. Annabel Lever explains: "pre-emptive racial profiling is controversial both because it is pre-emptive – no known illegal act has yet been committed – and because of the racial component in the decision to intervene" (Lever 2016). A compounding factor stems from the ways in which racial profiling has been practiced historically; past practice suggests a history of security authorities relying on questionable data to indicate that a particular religious or racial group is more likely to perpetrate a particular harm. No one doubts that racial profiling is clearly problematic when the racial profile is guided by racial animus rather than evidence.

But the more challenging philosophical question occurs when racial information is plausibly an element of a criminal profile, which can be used to efficiently allocate security resources toward high-risk targets. In this case, the racial information need not even be a particularly strong part of the profile; it must simply be the case that, on purely utilitarian grounds, there is an efficiency achieved by focusing disproportionately (but not exclusively) on members of the targeted racial group. However, even where based on genuine evidence rather than racial animus, racial profiling can be problematic for the ways in which it serves to compound disadvantage: "pre-emptive racial profiling seems particularly likely to reinforce racist beliefs about groups, by fostering misplaced claims about the causal importance of race in criminal behaviour" (Lever 2016). In other words, where racial minorities suffer disadvantage, the choice to profile them – even where some evidence suggests that doing so has benefits – can further disadvantage them, by signaling to others that they have greater proclivities toward wrongdoing *because* of their racial markers (rather than, for example, the systematic structural injustice to which they are subject).

This analysis highlights the importance, in what follows, of remaining attentive to the possibility that the alleged value of a particular policy, which targets disadvantaged minorities, is based in racial animus rather than evidence. It highlights, as well, that care must be taken even where evidence suggests that there may be security benefits to targeting disadvantaged minorities. The costs to already disadvantaged minorities of being targeted by counter-terror policies are high – higher than they might be for others who are not as disadvantaged, and possibly too high in a democratic state focused on protecting their equal status as citizens.

Contextual factors will need to be considered in any individual case, certainly, but the lesson here is to take seriously the additional costs imposed on disadvantaged minorities *when* they are selected for the rights constraints or restrictions demanded by the imperative to protect collective security. When they are targeted unfairly – when the transparency and proportionality requirements are not met – their entitlement to equal treatment is undermined. With these introductory comments as background, on the legitimacy of racial profiling in very general terms, the next two sections consider specific policies that, in their application, rely on what some believe is problematic racial profiling in order to determine who is subject to them.

No-Exit Policies and the Right to Move

Foreign fighters are individuals who reside or possess citizenship in one state and who choose to travel to foreign countries to join their wars. There are foreign fighters in every war – motivated by ideological reasons, often, as well as by promises of financial reward and a desire for adventure. George Orwell is perhaps one of the most famous of these. He fought in the Spanish Civil War, and then wrote *Homage to Catalonia* about the experience. Even though many legal systems do make it illegal to participate in other countries' wars, historically not much political attention has been given to foreign fighters, who have not generally been understood as a national security threat (de Roy van Zuijdewijn and Bakker 2004). Contemporary worries about foreign fighting stem from the seemingly large number of individuals from western, democratic states who have traveled to join ISIS, in fighting for a so-called "Islamic caliphate."

Democratic states have at least two distinct worries about foreign fighters (Webb 2017). One worry is that their radicalized citizens will travel abroad and participate in criminal activities. A second and distinct worry is that citizens will travel abroad, become (further) radicalized and return home with the intent and ability to harm fellow citizens. The fact of foreign fighters – both those who travel abroad and those who return or attempt to return home – has generated a range of policies, aimed at reducing the outflow of foreign fighters from democratic states, as well as reducing the likelihood that those who return home engage in harm. This section considers only the former policies, targeted at reducing the outflow of foreign fighters. Two specific policies are the target of analysis here: so-called "no-fly lists" – lists of individuals who are not permitted to board airplanes – and passport cancellations (Lenard 2014). These policies all reduce the ability of individuals to move across borders; in particular, they target the right to exit a state, which is acknowledged as fundamental by the Universal Declaration of Human Rights (United Nations 1948).

The US no-fly list is perhaps the most well known of such lists, though they are in operation in many countries, including the UK, Australia and Canada. In the United States, the no-fly list is composed of two separate lists, one of which identifies individuals who are not permitted to fly, and the second of which lists individuals who may be permitted to fly, but who are subject to additional security screening before they are permitted to board a flight (it is termed the "selectee" list). The lists were created following the terrorist attacks on US soil in 2001.

Passport cancellations, or non-renewals, operate differently. Usually, passport cancellations are deployed to prevent individuals from exiting their state, though they are also used to prevent individuals from re-entering their state of citizenship. In many cases, cancelling a passport of an individual who is abroad is understood to be equivalent to revoking their citizenship; citizenship revocation was considered in chapter 2, and in this section, this use of passport cancellation will be set aside (but see Weil 2013). As part of the global fight against terrorism, many states have adopted explicit legislation permitting – and even requiring – the cancellation of passports of individuals believed to be intending to join foreign wars, or to participate in terrorist activities abroad. For example, in Canada, at least since the 2004 Canadian Passport Order, the government has possessed the power to revoke the passports of individuals traveling abroad where it "has reasonable grounds to suspect that the decision is necessary to prevent the commission of a terrorism offence . . . or for the national security of Canada or a foreign country or state" (Government of Canada 2019). Similarly, Australia has recently adopted legislation that specifically permits the revocation of passports of those suspected of desiring to join terrorist groups abroad; estimates suggest that 240 Australian passports have been cancelled or denied to individuals who are suspected of wanting to join the conflicts in Iraq and Syria (Wood 2018).

The security test applied to no-exit policies

The security test first asks whether there is a real threat to basic security to be confronted. The global commitment to combat terror, and the imperative that states protect their own jurisdiction from terrorism, means that states must do what they can to ensure that their own citizens do not travel to commit acts of terror. Additionally, returning foreign fighters not only may be radicalized, they may return with the resources they need to threaten the basic institutions of a democratic state. Most western states have seen an outflow of foreign fighters; and most are now confronting their return including whether to allow it and how to treat them, if they do. UN estimates suggest that 40,000 foreign fighters, from 110 countries, may have participated in the conflict in Iraq and Syria (UN Press Release 2017); many have been captured or killed, but many others are returning, or attempting to do so. The threat of foreign fighters and the harm that they can do, abroad and upon return home, is legitimately worrying (Canadian Security Intelligence Service 2016; *CNN* Editorial Research 2019).

The second question directs attention toward the cost of a particular policy, with respect to the rights constraints and restrictions it imposes. No-fly lists and passport cancellations target the right to exit one's state. The right to exit one's state (no reason needs to be given) is generally understood to be one of the most basic of human rights, for its role in giving citizens a mechanism to escape an oppressive state (Lenard 2015; Whelan 1981). The right to exit can also be understood as one component of the more general right to move freely, in pursuit of one's objectives. This more expansive right to move may be subject to more constraints than the right to exit, but it is nevertheless an essential basic right; one must be able to move freely to pursue relationships that one values, to engage in political activity, to pursue educational and employment opportunities. In many cases, pursuing these goods will require crossing borders (Oberman 2016). The key role that the right to move plays in living a basic or flourishing human life suggests that the willingness to restrict a citizen's right to exit her state, without compelling reason to do so, should be understood as a grave harm.

This acknowledgment does not mean there are never reasons to constrain or restrict movement. For example, criminals do not have the right to escape prosecution, and so can reasonably be denied the right to cross borders. However, those who are placed on no-fly lists, or whose passports are cancelled, are not necessarily – or even usually – people who have committed crimes; rather, they are individuals who are *suspected* of desiring to do so. Many people who are affected – if not most – will simply be people who are aiming to travel to controversial locations, for deeply important personal reasons, including to attend weddings and funerals, and to pursue time-sensitive job opportunities.

In other words, at issue is not whether criminals can be denied the right to travel (they can be), but rather how those who are *pre-emptively* denied the right to travel are selected. Many have observed that those whose rights are restricted appear disproportionately to be visible minority individuals with cultural or religious connections to Islam (e.g., Nagra and Maurutto, 2019). The result of these additional security assessments, imposed on Muslim-appearing individuals, is the public perception that these citizens are indeed worthy of suspicion, just as many have worried (Lever 2016; Hosein 2018).

One might respond by noting that there is good reason for the public perception that Muslim-appearing individuals are worthy of suspicion. After all, the perpetrators of many well-known terrorist incidents claim to be Muslim, including the perpetrators of the attacks at the *Charlie Hebdo* offices and the Bataclan Theatre in Paris, both in 2015, and the shooting at the Jewish Museum of Brussels in 2014 and the bombings in Brussels in 2016, at the airport and on the metro. These highly publicized incidents of terrorism are horrendous, but it is crucial to keep in mind that the vast majority of individuals who share the religious or ethnic traits of those who committed these crimes are not terrorists and have no sympathy with terrorist actions allegedly committed in the name of Islam (Hellyer 2019; Strickland 2019).

Perhaps one thinks, however, that statistics bear out the claim that Muslim-appearing individuals are worthy of suspicion. For example, in the United States, of the over 100 domestic incidents classified as terrorism between the years 2010 and 2016, 30 percent were connected to Islamic or jihadist terror (START 2017). Since just under 1 percent of the US population is Muslim, the fact that they commit 30 percent of the terrorist attacks in the US suggests that a random Muslim in America is 30 times more likely than an average American to be a terrorist. This statistic justifies Muslims appearing on no-fly lists in greater proportion than their fraction of the general population. In other words, it is not their (apparent) over-inclusion as visible counter-terror targets that generates suspicions of Muslim and Muslim-appearing citizens and residents; rather, it is that members of this community are in fact responsible for so many more terrorist attacks, proportionally speaking, that is the source of the generalized suspicion of such individuals.

This use of the statistics is not the right way to think about the issue at stake, however. Consider a well-focused and unbiased crime-prevention program. In this scenario, the expectation is that the fraction of people drawn into that program who are members of any group should be roughly the same as the fraction of criminals who are members of that group. That is, if the program is targeting people without bias, the targets of a crime-prevention program should match the proportion of *criminals*, not the proportion of the general population. So, if Muslims commit 30 percent of terrorist acts, one would expect approximately 30 percent of the people targeted by any given counter-terror program to be Muslim. If a counter-terror program has 80 percent of its targets from the Muslim community, there would be reason to believe that the program is biased (as a matter of fact, the composition of no-fly lists is not publicly known).

Or, look at the question in another way. As noted above, from 2010 to 2016, there were approximately 100 terrorist attacks committed in the US. This means that, in a seven-year span, approximately 1 in 3 million people committed a terrorist act. So, if you pick a random American and wonder whether she is a terrorist, you should expect about a 1-in-3-million chance that she is. If that person is a Muslim, those odds are still only 1 in 100,000, which is to say that 99,999 of every 100,000 Muslims are not terrorists. These numbers may (or may not) warrant the focus of counter-terrorism efforts, but they certainly suggest that the suspicion of Muslims evidenced by general populations stems from somewhere *other than* the risk such citizens actually pose to security. The point of this analysis is, simply, that the impact of security-focused policies on those who are highly statistically likely to be innocent *matters*.

The third prong of the security test directs focus onto the transparency of the adoption and application of a particular policy. Travel restriction policies have been plagued with a lack of transparency in their implementation, in two related ways: with respect to who is *on* the list; and, when one is on the list in error, how one can be removed from it. Often, the way people find out either that they are on a no-fly list, or that their passport has been cancelled, is by attempting to check in for a flight and learning that they may not board (Luongo 2016; Jamil 2017). The evidence that has been gathered to justify travel restrictions of these kinds is not easily accessible, and the agencies involved have not provided transparent and clear accounting of the reasons for which individuals are selected for restrictions. The International Civil Liberties Monitoring Group has specifically objected to Canada's no-fly list, for example, by noting that it "undermines the right to due process for individuals on the list through a lack of transparency and access to information" (Jarvis 2018). Indeed, when the Office of the Information Commissioner (2016) asked the Canadian Federal Court to require Transport Canada (which manages Canada's no-fly list) to release information about who is on the list, and how many of these individuals are Canadian, its request was denied.

Lack of transparency with respect to who is on the list is compounded by the challenges in accessing redress, should one be denied the right to renew a passport, or to fly. The absence of accessible procedures across democratic states for determining that one is on the list, and then combatting this status, is problematic not only for the way in which it undermines the right to exit one's state, but also for the ways in which it subjects citizens to such a violation – often humiliating because announced in public spaces – without offering the recourse to which one is entitled as a member of a democratic community, who has not been convicted or even accused of criminal wrongdoing. The most famous cases of individuals flagged on the no-fly list are of toddlers whose names are said to match those of would-be or actual terrorists, but the reality is that many, if not most, adults on the lists are believed to be there for similarly mistaken reasons, and achieving redress, though it has been promised to be available, has proven difficult if not impossible (Jamil 2017).

So, the security test tells us that, while there are legitimate reasons to worry about the outflow, and return, of foreign fighters, the costs of travel restrictions, and the lack of transparency in their implementation, render them problematic in their present incarnation. The first step to rendering them justified is to focus on mending the redress procedures so that those who are mistakenly subject to travel restrictions can be freed to travel as quickly as possible. Redress mechanisms will not serve to reduce the stigmatization connected to boarding refusals, or the intensive pre-boarding security checks that nevertheless result in boarding, however. One possible strategy to avoid the humiliation of boarding refusals, as well as additional, secondary, screening, may be to encourage the use of advanced screening techniques such as trusted traveler programs, which permit travelers to participate in security screening in advance so that, at the time of travel, their movement through airports and security checks is smooth. An advantage of such a strategy – perhaps adopted pre-emptively by airlines in collaboration with security agencies, to alert passengers that they should take advantage of such programs – is that it permits greater transparency for those subject to possible movement restrictions, allowing them to present evidence that their movement does not pose threats. Moreover, it reduces the threat of public humiliation that is connected to being selected for additional security screening.

Surveillance and the Right to Privacy

Citizens are subject to surveillance in myriad forms. Government agencies across democratic countries monitor telephone usage, they track internet usage patterns, biometric data are increasingly collected, and so on. There are multiple programs across democratic states that permit or require the gathering of data around how citizens behave in public spaces and online, including what websites they visit and what they post to social media. These data can be used by security authorities to seek patterns in internet usage that could suggest terrorist affiliations, and so warrant further scrutiny (Taylor 2018, 30). The precise challenges these surveillance techniques present, morally speaking, are contextual – for example, some techniques subject large numbers of citizens to surveillance, and others only a small number; and some techniques subject citizens to surveillance in public spaces only, whereas others also target private spaces.

To assess some of the challenges, consider Prevent, a British surveillance program in operation since 2002 that "aims to stop people becoming terrorists or supporting terrorism" (UK Home Office 2019). Prevent's objective is to identify individuals who can benefit from deradicalization programs, and then to provide them with access to a range of social services (education, counseling, and so on), which can be of value to recipients beyond their role in helping them avoid radicalization. Legislative changes enacted in the 2015 Counter-Terrorism and Security Act imposed a "prevent duty" on a range of public-sector workers to identify and refer individuals believed to be at risk of radicalization to Prevent authorities (Dudenhoefer 2018). As a result of its wide reach, a young person in the UK interacts with several Prevent reporters – including educators and health-care providers – on a daily basis, making the surveillance it imposes both widespread and personal.

The security test applied to Prevent's duty to report

The first dimension of the security test considers whether the proposed policy aims at protecting basic security. In the case of Prevent's form of surveillance, the main objective is to detect would-be terrorists, before they take harmful actions, and then to offer them targeted support. The aim of intervening to stop radicalization is justifiably a key component of any state's efforts to protect its basic security, so it passes this requirement.

The security test focuses, second, on the question of proportionality. What are the costs generated by Prevent's duty to report? In very general terms, surveillance interrupts the right to privacy, understood broadly to mean an individual's right to live her life without being observed by others. It is meant to protect citizens from intrusion on their private lives; citizens have strong interests in being able to make personal and political choices without worry that they are being scrutinized (Taylor 2018, ch. 2). The duty to report interrupts the right to privacy in an unusual way, by requiring public actors to evaluate many personal and political choices – many of which are ostensibly *private* – of those in their care. Just to give some examples: public actors are instructed that changes in physical appearance, religious commitment and friendship groups can be signs of radicalization (HM Government 2015, 47–54); all of these are choices protected by the right to privacy (and perhaps other rights as well).

Why might people worry about being referred to Prevent? After all, as described above, the referral can often be accompanied by access to specialized social services, which may be thought valuable. Multiple worries have been expressed about the harms of referral, however, including the harm of stigma generated by the referral itself; of the questioning by security authorities; of the additional scrutiny of family members; of the possibly permanent recording of the referral in official security-authority databases, and so on (Anderson 2015; Grierson 2019). Fears of referral are thus generating a "chilling effect" among those who believe they are at risk of being referred – that is, they respond to these fears by changing their behaviors in ways they believe will reduce the likelihood that they come to the attention of public authorities (Hosein 2018). So, consider cases where Muslims worry

> that articulating a particular opinion or involving oneself in politics and/or dissent may lead one to be viewed as a suspected terrorist. In such an instance, students begin to self-discipline and self-censor their behavior, thoughts and actions. Whilst Prevent may not therefore entail a direct exercise of force, say arrest and detention, through the threat of some "potential action" being taken, it indirectly threatens individuals and produces outcomes that arrest and detention do – fear, anxiety and disengagement. (Sabir 2016, 11)

In other words, the way in which the duty to report, as a form of surveillance, interrupts the right to make choices about one's private life is by generating worry about being reported that is so severe that individuals make choices they would not otherwise make.

One might ask whether British Muslims are right to believe they are (disproportionately) at risk of being reported. In justifying the program, defenders observe that it aims at identifying both those at risk of far-right radicalization and those at risk of religious extremist violence. In 2017–18, of the people who received Prevent support, 45 percent had been referred for concerns about Islamic terrorism, and 44 percent had been referred for concerns about far-right extremism (UK Home Office 2018).

However, the difficulty lies not with the small population of individuals who receive support, but rather with the significantly larger number of individuals who are referred by public actors to Prevent authorities in the first place. Even though individuals receiving Prevent support are evenly divided between these two populations, in 2017–18 there were almost two and a half times as many initial referrals of Muslims as of potential far-right actors. So, while Prevent authorities (so-called "Channel Panels"[1]) appear able to recognize many of these referrals as being baseless, the disparity in referrals suggests the presence of bias among public actors, whose generalized suspicions of Muslim citizens appear to have had an impact in guiding their choices of whom to refer (Rights Watch UK 2016; Cohen and Tufail 2017). These disparities suggest, say Prevent's critics, that the duty to report encourages public-sector workers to engage in racial profiling – i.e. to view statements and actions in chil-

---

[1] Channel panels are the panels that assess whether referred cases warrant further assessment. A separate question is whether these evaluators are bias-free.

dren and other young people as suspicious if they are made by Muslims, even when they would be viewed as innocuous (and thereby not raise suspicions) if made by non-Muslims. It is no wonder, then, that Muslims are suspicious of the Prevent program, believing that it operates fundamentally on the basis of racial hostility rather than good evidence (UK Home Affairs Committee 2016, 18; Qurashi 2018).

The third component of the security test directs attention toward questions of transparency. Questions of transparency in the case of the duty to report focus on whether it is effective at doing its job, i.e., of properly identifying individuals at risk of radicalization and offering them the services they require. Defenders of the program point to the number of individuals who are receiving support (Dearden 2019a). Its critics point to widely mocked cases – for example, of a 4-year old boy being referred to a de-radicalization program for drawing a picture of his father cutting a cucumber, which was misunderstood as a picture of his father making a "cooker bomb" (Quinn 2016) – and more troubling ones, including students who appear to be of Middle Eastern background being reported to Prevent authorities when engaging in perfectly normal and expected learning activities – for example, completing assigned readings on "terrorism" for relevant courses – in high schools and universities (Sabir 2016).

The UK government announced its intent in January 2019 to conduct an independent review of Prevent, in part to assess whether it is doing its job as intended (Dearden 2019a). More generally, the question of the *effectiveness* of counter-terror policies, including Prevent, matters with regard to whether they can be justified. Note, however, that effectiveness is not a simple concept – that is to say, in order to know whether a policy is effective, the objectives of the policy must be clearly set out, with pre-identified indicators that will support post-implementation evaluation; this is part of the transparency requirement.

Additionally, as the security test is meant to indicate, the question of whether a policy is effective is not simply a matter of achieving an objective, but of assessing the costs associated with achieving this objective. So, the anticipated independent review of Prevent will require that its objectives be evaluated against its results, alongside an assessment of the costs of carrying it out, on those who are most affected.[2]

---

[2] At the time of writing, some concerns were being voiced that the review is not being conducted in a way that will give its critics the information they need to be reassured about its operation (Dearden 2019b).

In its present incarnation, Prevent's duty to report does not pass the security test. The objective is an important one – i.e., to identify individuals at risk of radicalization and to offer them the services they need to reject it. However, the surveillance demanded by Prevent is unique, in the way it monitors people's everyday lives through their interactions with the public sector; it has been described as the most intrusive of surveillance policies adopted in democratic states. Although it focuses on identifying all forms of extremists, the costs imposed on especially Muslim communities, in the form of implicitly encouraging public-sector workers to act on their bias rather than suppress it (and as a result subjecting many innocent Muslims to intrusive and embarrassing examinations by Prevent authorities), have so far been too high to countenance the intrusions. Every day, people are normally subject to multiple forms of surveillance, physically and online; but, where surveillance targets are selected in ways that demonstrate, encourage and foster racial animus, as appears to be the case with respect to Prevent's duty to report, they are unjustified.

Conclusion

States must focus on preventing terrorism every day, and they have adopted multiple strategies to do so. These policies can often be justified for the benefits they bring to a state's basic security, even when they do so by imposing costs on citizens. But, this is not always, or even often, the case. This chapter began by proposing a security test to use for assessing whether the security benefit that is produced by a particular policy can be justified to those who bear its costs. This test asks whether the security benefit is real; whether the costs imposed on citizens are proportionate; and whether the justifications for the policy and its applications are made in a transparent way. The test was applied to three kinds of policies: those that expand the domain of prohibited speech; those that restrict travel; and those that subject some or all citizens to surveillance. In some cases, particular policies target some but not all citizens for additional costs; the chapter has examined when this narrow targeting can be permissible, and has encouraged attention to cases where this targeting may be the result of racial animus. The worry that racial animus guides selecting targets is especially strong where Muslim communities bear the costs of a particular prevention policy, and these heightened costs may render a particular policy unjustified according to the dictates of the security test.

Concluding Remarks

There is no doubt that protecting citizens from terrorist threats must be a priority for all states, including democratic ones. One source of a state's legitimacy is its capacity to protect all those in its jurisdiction, and the range of policies that a state adopts to do so is vast. This book has examined two broad categories of policies that a state can adopt to combat terrorism: policies to punish terrorist wrongdoers, and policies to prevent terrorist wrongdoing. In each case, so the argument has gone, a democratic state is constrained not simply by the import of protecting the basic human rights of citizens and residents on its territory, but also by the imperative to protect *equality* among them. That is, any security-protecting policy must aim not only at protecting security directly, but also at protecting the equality of citizens on an equal basis.

This equality is realized in the form of equal protection of rights for all citizens, including victims and perpetrators of terrorism, as well as the many others whose lives are touched directly by policies to protect states against terrorism.

This book opened with a caution against thinking of security in narrow terms, as referring only to the protection of a community's overall security, understood exclusively or mainly in physical terms. Security is a complex concept: a community is secure to the extent that its citizens are relatively free from physical threats, certainly. But, as has been elaborated through this book, there is much more to security. For one thing, security is as much a collective or public good as it is a feature of individuals. So, it makes sense to describe communities as secure or insecure, and individuals as secure or insecure. As well, security has objective and subjective components. A community or an individual may be objectively secure, as assessed with respect to rate of crime, or violence to which they may be subject. And a community or an individual may feel secure or insecure, even when according to certain objective measures they perhaps ought to feel differently. A person who is at low risk of violence at the hands of others may nevertheless believe herself to be at significant risk of this violence, and a person at significant risk may believe herself to be at low risk. Moreover, chapter 1 noted, security exists on a continuum: both communities and individuals can be more or less secure, and no individual, and no community, can be perfectly secure.

All of the complexities that travel with the term "security" make it hard to understand how and when to prioritize it, and so this book also cautioned against treating "security" as though it can be balanced in a straightforward way against "rights," as has sometimes been suggested. Rather, any assessment of when to prioritize security over rights is in fact an assessment of when to prioritize which form of security (individual, collective, subjective, objective) over which specific right or set of rights.

Chapter 2 asked how democracies can fairly and justly punish terrorists. The challenge in doing so stems from the nature of terrorists, who in the cases considered in this book are individuals who question the very foundations of democratic states. In particular, they are individuals who, by their actions, intend to attack the values, and also the institutions, that support democratic practice among a diverse citizenry, by instilling fear in that citizenry. For some, such individuals merit exclusion from the state that they desired, or attempted, to undermine;

the exclusion they lobby for is often permanent, in the form of life sentences or forced exile. But, the book has proposed, a commitment to democratic principles requires treating even the most heinous of individuals – Bowers, Breivik and other terrorists who survived their crimes – at least in principle, as capable of re-entering the democratic fold, and so it has advocated against all forms of *permanent* punishment. It defended the application of terrorist sentencing enhancements and hate crime penalties, however, in cases where terrorists aimed by their actions to instill fear among citizens, especially (but not limited to) those who are disadvantaged. These penalties signal a state's willingness to recognize – even where perpetrators of certain crimes do not – the fundamental equality of all citizens.

Chapter 3 considered policies that democracies adopt over the long term to combat terrorism, rather than those adopted in the face of an imminent, credible, violent threat, or recent terrorist incident. Policies to prevent terror that are in place over an extended period of time can, in some cases, appear to prioritize collective security over the rights of individuals in a democratic state. Any persistent rights constraint, adopted in the name of security, must be interrogated, this book has argued. To do so, it proposed a simple "security test," which can be deployed as a diagnostic tool, to assess whether a proposed policy is genuinely aimed at protecting *basic* and *fundamental* security; whether the costs imposed on particular individuals or communities are proportional to the security gains anticipated; and whether the adoption of the policy, and the implementation of the policy, are properly transparent.

There is always a caveat here, lurking at the back of many people's minds: what if these rights constraints, though frustrating for some individuals, save a *life*? Isn't it right to say, in such a situation, that the rights constraints in such a situation are a relatively minor cost to bear? Those who defend robust terrorism-prevention policies, with an emphasis on only the physical security of citizens and residents, argue that these costs are insubstantial compared to the goods that are gained, and public opinion often seems to support this sort of view. This proposal fails to recognize how often democratic states adopt policies that "sacrifice" lives in favor of protecting certain rights: a simple example is the willingness of democratic states to permit relatively high speed limits, knowing that decreases in these limits will save lives. In any case, chapter 1's objective was to tackle this simplistic way of thinking through the dilemmas in fact posed by security policies of various kinds. The applica tion of the security test highlights the importance of evaluating, and reevaluating, policies that, in the name of security, impose persistent, long-term constraints or restrictions of rights, on all, or only some, citizens. Many terrorism prevention policies *select* individuals or groups of individuals for rights constraints and restrictions, and democratic states must be on guard that those targeted are fairly selected. In many cases considered in this book, unfortunately, discrimination against a minority group travels with the demand that this same community bear the costs of counter-terrorism policies, costs that are sometimes substantial. For these disadvantaged groups, the costs include: an increased likelihood of having a right constrained or restricted; the felt requirement that, to avoid coming to the attention of authorities, they must alter the way in which they exercise key rights, including rights to associate and religious expression; and being on the receiving end of the generalized suspicion from fellow citizens that such policies can create.

The fact of systemic discrimination makes it easier to neglect the rights of those who bear the costs of terrorism-prevention policies, costs which may be thereby unjustly demanded of disadvantaged minority communities. Moreover, these policies may also fail to be effective, since they may rely implicitly or explicitly on the cooperation of those who bear their costs; this cooperation may not be readily extended where these costs are believed to be unfairly imposed – that is, absent good evidence and under conditions of secrecy rather than transparency.

This is what the examination of Prevent, in chapter 3, suggested. The security test's emphasis on the proportionality of specific prevention policies, as well as on their transparency, is aimed at remedying these possible pitfalls of terrorism-prevention policies: it asks that the choice of whom to select for prevention policies is made transparent, and they ask that proof be furnished that these policies are the *least costly* available to generate the anticipated security benefit. This security benefit must, moreover, be real rather than imagined, and evidence must be provided to this effect. Evidence can be collected in myriad ways: by assessing how related policies have worked in other jurisdictions; by adopting policies on a small scale to assess their effectiveness, before adopting them more widely; by ensuring that policies are adopted with a clause requiring that, after a certain period of time, they are evaluated for effectiveness before being permitted to persist over the longer term.

And so, this book has argued, engaging in the fiction that it is easy and straightforward to balance rights and security is both harmful and counterproductive. Doing so can threaten to undermine the rights of all citizens, especially disadvantaged minorities, for little security benefit; on the contrary, long-term, persistent, rights constraints and restrictions, targeted at disadvantaged minorities, threaten both the egalitarianism to which democracies are meant to be committed and, as a result, their security.

There is a larger worry, as well. Where disadvantaged minorities are subject to unjustified rights constraints and restrictions, their commitment to the collaborative practices that underpin many security policies may wane; correspondingly, the withdrawal of minority citizens from collaborative democratic practice in the domain of security must, going forward, be treated as a major *security failure* in democratic states. To repeat, by way of conclusion, it is a failure not simply because citizens' rights are targeted for constraints and restrictions absent evidence that this is good policy – though this is bad enough in democratic states. It is a failure, ultimately, because it threatens to spur the withdrawal of the cooperation that is essential for protecting the collective security to which all citizens are entitled.

References

Anderson, David. 2015. "The Terrorism Acts in 2014: Report of the Independent Reviewer of the Operation of the Terrorism Act 2000 and Part 1 of the Terrorism Act 2006." https://assets.publishing.service.gov.uk/government/uploads/system/uploads/attachment_data/file/461404/6_1256_EL_The_Terrorism_Act_Report_2015_FINAL_16_0915_WEB.pdf.

Anderson, Elizabeth. 1999. "What Is the Point of Equality?" *Ethics* 109 (2): 287–337.

Arendt, Hannah. 1963. *Eichmann in Jerusalem*. London: Penguin.

Baldwin, David A. 1997. "The Concept of Security." *Review of International Studies* 23: 5–26.

Barendt, Eric. 2009. "Incitement to, and Glorification of, Terrorism." In *Extreme Speech and Democracy*, edited by Ivan Hare and James Weinstein, 445–62. Oxford University Press.

References

BBC News. 2012. "Norway Attacks: Breivik Charged with Terror Attacks." March 7. www.bbc.com/news/world-europe-17286154.

Blake, Michael. 2001. "Distributive Justice, State Coercion, and Autonomy." *Philosophy & Public Affairs* 30 (3): 257–96.

Busby, Mattha. 2018. "UK Has Not 'Woken Up' to Far-Right Threat, Says Ex-Counter-Terror Chief." *The Guardian*, August 18. www.theguardian.com/uk-news/2018/aug/18/former-counter-terrorism-chief-says-uk-has-not-woken-up-to-far-right-threat.

Canadian Security Intelligence Service. 2016. "The Foreign Fighters Phenomenon and Related Security Trends in the Middle East." World Watch Expert Notes, www.canada.ca/content/dam/csis-scrs/documents/publications/20160129-en.pdf.

Chavez, Nicole, Emanuella Grinberg and Eliott C. McLaughlin. 2018. "Pittsburgh Synagogue Gunman Said He Wanted All Jews to Die, Criminal Complaint Says." *CNN*, October 31. www.cnn.com/2018/10/28/us/pittsburgh-synagogue-shooting/index.html.

Choudhury, Tufyal. 2009. "The Terrorism Act 2006: Discouraging Terrorism." In *Extreme Speech and Democracy*, edited by Ivan Hare and James Weinstein, 463–87. Oxford University Press.

CNN Editorial Research. 2019. "2015 Paris Terror Attacks Fast Facts." CNN Online, November 13.

www.cnn.com/2015/12/08/europe/2015-paris-terror-attacks-fast-facts/index.html.

Coady, C. A. J. 1985. "The Morality of Terrorism." *Philosophy* 60: 47–69.

Cohen, Barbara, and Waqas Tufail. 2017. "Prevent and the Normalization of Islamophobia." In *Islamophobia: Still a Challenge for Us All*, 41–5. London: Runnymede Trust.

Cohen, Elizabeth F. 2016. "When Democracies Denationalize: The Epistemological Case against Revoking Citizenship." *Ethics & International Affairs* 30 (2): 253–9.

Dearden, Lizzie. 2019a. "UK's Prevent Counter-Extremism Programme to Be Independently Reviewed." *The Independent*, January 22. www.independent.co.uk/news/uk/home-news/terror-uk-prevent-review-independent-counter-terrorism-border-security-bill-muslims-a8741306.html.

Dearden, Lizzie. 2019b. "Review of Prevent Counter-Extremism Scheme Risks Becoming 'Whitewashed' Government Warned." *The Independent*, August 10. www.independent.co.uk/news/uk/home-news/extremism-muslims-spying-far-right-human-rights-review-a9050666.html.

Drury, Colin. 2019. "Isis Bride Says She Was Brainwashed and Wants Second Chance." *The Independent*, April 2. www.independent.co.uk/news/uk/home-news/shamima-begum-isis-bride-interview-baby-death-syria-isla mic-state-a8850291.html.

Dudenhoefer, Anne-Lynn. 2018. "Resisting Radicalisation: A Critical Analysis of the UK Prevent Duty." *Journal for Deradicalization* 14: 153–91.

Duff, Antony. 2009. "Can We Punish the Perpetrators of Atrocities?" In *The Religious in Responses to Mass Atrocity: Interdisciplinary Perspectives*, edited by Thomas Brudholm and Thomas Cushman, 79–104. Cambridge University Press.

Dworkin, Ronald. 1981. "Is There a Right to Pornography?" *Oxford Journal of Legal Studies* 1 (2): 177–212. https://doi.org/10.1093/ojls/1.2.177.

Ferracioli, Luara. 2017. "Citizenship Allocation and Withdrawal: Some Normative Issues." *Philosophy Compass* 12 (12): 1–9.

Fisher, Max. 2012. "A Different Justice: Why Anders Breivik Only Got 21 Years for Killing 77 People." *The Atlantic*, August 24. www.theatlantic.com/internatio nal/archive/2012/08/a-different-justice-why-anders-br eivik-only-got-21-years-for-killing-77-people/261532.

Forsdyke, Sara. 2009. *Exile, Ostracism, and Democracy: The Politics of Expulsion in Ancient Greece.* Princeton University Press.

Fung, Archon. 2013. "Infotopia: Unleashing the Democratic Power of Transparency." *Politics & Society* 41 (2): 183–212.

Gelber, Katharine. 2019. "Terrorist–Extremist Speech and Hate Speech: Understanding the Similarities and

Differences." *Ethical Theory and Moral Practice*, online early.

Gibney, Matthew J. 2013. "'A Very Transcendental Power': Denaturalisation and the Liberalisation of Citizenship in the United Kingdom." *Political Studies* 61 (3): 637–55.

Government of Canada. 2017. "National Security Transparency Commitment." www.canada.ca/en/ser vices/defence/nationalsecurity/national-security-trans parency-commitment.html.

Government of Canada. 2019. "Canadian Passport Order," last amended May 2019. https://laws.justice. gc.ca/PDF/SI-81-86.pdf.

Grierson, Jamie. 2019. "Database 'reinforces worst fears' about Prevent, says Labour." *The Guardian*, October 7. www.theguardian.com/uk-news/2019/oct/ 07/secret-prevent-index-reinforces-worst-fears-about-programme.

Groot, Gerard-René de, and Maarten P. Vink. 2010. "Loss of Citizenship: Trends and Regulations in Europe." EUDO Citizenship Observatory, Robert Schuman Centre for Advanced Studies, European University Institute. http://eudo-citizenship.eu/docs/ Loss.pdf.

Hadjimatheou, Katerina. 2014. "The Relative Moral Risks of Untargeted and Targeted Surveillance." *Ethical Theory and Moral Practice* 17 (2): 187–207.

Hall, Richard, and Lizzie Dearden. 2019. "Shamima Begum 'Was Member of Feared Isis Morality Police' in Syria." *The Independent*, April 14. www.independent.co.uk/news/world/middle-east/shamima-begum-isis-syria-morality-police-suicide-belts-a8869016.html.

Hankes, Keegan, Rachel Janik and Michael Edison Heyden. 2019. "Shooting at Poway Synagogue Underscores Link Between Internet Radicalization and Violence." Southern Poverty Law Center. www.splcenter.org/hatewatch/2019/04/28/shooting-poway-synagogue-underscores-link-between-internet-radicalization-and-violence.

Hellyer, H. A. 2019. "Where We Go Wrong in Comparing White Supremacy With ISIS." *Time*, March 21. https://time.com/5555845/white-supremacy-isis-threat-west.

HM Government. 2015. "Channel Duty Guidance: Protecting Vulnerable People from Being Drawn into Terrorism." https://assets.publishing.service.gov.uk/government/uploads/system/uploads/attachment_data/file/425189/Channel_Duty_Guidance_April_2015.pdf.

Hosein, Adam Omar. 2018. "Racial Profiling and a Reasonable Sense of Inferior Political Status." *Journal of Political Philosophy* 26 (3): e1–20.

Ignatieff, Michael. 2004. *The Lesser Evil: Political Ethics in an Age of Terror*. Toronto: Penguin Canada.

Ivandic, Ria, Tom Kirchmaier and Stephen Machin. 2019. "Jihadi Attacks, Media, and Local Anti-Muslim

Hate Crime." *Vox*, September 6, https://voxeu.org/article/jihadi-attacks-media-and-local-anti-muslim-hate-crime

Jamil, Uzma. 2017. "Can Muslims Fly? The No Fly List as a Tool of the 'War on Terror.'" *Islamophobia Studies Journal* 4 (1): 73–86.

Jarvis, Amelia. 2018. "Canada's No Fly List." International Civil Liberties Monitoring Group (blog). https://iclmg.ca/issues/canadas-no-fly-list.

Joppke, Christian. 2016. "Terror and the Loss of Citizenship." *Citizenship Studies* 20 (6–7): 728–48.

Kingston, Rebecca. 2005. "The Unmaking of Citizens: Banishment and the Modern Citizenship Regime in France." *Citizenship Studies* 9 (1): 23–40.

Lazar, Nomi Claire. 2009. *States of Emergency in Liberal Democracies*. Cambridge University Press.

Lenard, Patti Tamara. 2012. *Trust, Democracy and Multicultural Challenges*. University Park, PA: Penn State Press.

Lenard, Patti Tamara. 2014. "Security and Migration." In *Human Rights, Human Security, and National Security*, edited by Saul Takahashi. Santa Barbara, CA: Praeger.

Lenard, Patti Tamara. 2015. "Exit and the Duty to Admit." *Ethics and Global Politics* 8. www.ethicsandglobalpolitics.net/index.php/egp/article/view/25975.

Lenard, Patti Tamara. 2016. "Democracies and the

Power to Revoke Citizenship." *Ethics & International Affairs* 30 (1): 73–91.

Lenard, Patti Tamara. 2018. "Democratic Citizenship and Denationalization." *American Political Science Review* 112 (1): 99–111.

Lenard, Patti Tamara. 2019. "Punishment or Banishment?" CIPS Blog (blog). February 22. www. cips-cepi.ca/2019/02/22/we-must-punish-our-own-ter rorists-not-revoke-their-citizenship.

Lenard, Patti Tamara, and Terry Macdonald. Forthcoming. "Democracy versus Security as Standards of Political Legitimacy: The Case of National Policy on Irregular Migrant Arrivals." *Perspectives on Politics.* https://doi.org/10.1017/S1537592719003402.

Lepoutre, Maxime. 2019. "Can 'More Speech' Counter Ignorant Speech?" *Journal of Ethics and Social Philosophy* 16 (3).

Lever, Annabel. 2016. "Racial Profiling and the Political Philosophy of Race." In *The Oxford Handbook of the Philosophy of Race*, edited by Naomi Zack, 425–35. Oxford University Press. www.oxfordhandbooks.com/ view/10.1093/oxfordhb/9780190236953.001.0001/ox fordhb-9780190236953-e-7.

Lewis, Mark, and Sarah Lyall. 2012. "Norway Mass Killer Gets the Maximum: 21 Years." *New York Times*, August 24. www.nytimes.com/2012/08/25/wo rld/europe/anders-behring-breivik-murder-trial.html.

Luongo, Michael T. 2016. "Traveling While Muslim

Complicates Air Travel." *New York Times*, November 7. www.nytimes.com/2016/11/08/business/traveling-while-muslim-complicates-air-travel.html.

Macklin, Audrey. 2014. "Citizenship Revocation, the Privilege to Have Rights and the Production of the Alien." *Queen's Law Journal* 40 (1): 1–54.

Meisels, Tamar. 2008. *The Trouble with Terror: Liberty, Security, and the Response to Terrorism*. Cambridge University Press.

Mill, John Stuart. 1991. *On Liberty and Other Essays*, edited by J. Gray. Oxford University Press.

Modood, Tariq. 2006. "The Liberal Dilemma: Integration or Vilification?" *International Migration* 44 (5): 4–7.

Nagin, Daniel S. 2013. "Deterrence in the Twenty-First Century." *Crime and Justice* 42: 199–263.

Nagra, Baljit, and Paula Maurutto. 2019. "No-Fly Lists, National Security and Race: The Experiences of Canadian Muslims." *British Journal of Criminology*, online early.

Newey, Glen. 2012. "Liberty, Security Notwithstanding." In *Social Cohesion, Securitization and Counter-Terrorism*, edited by Charles Husband, 1–21. Helsinki Collegium for Advanced Studies.

Newheiser, Anna, and Tina DeMarco. 2018. "Who Deserves Civil Rights? Many Say Suspected Terrorists Do Not." *Law and Human Behavior* 42 (1): 50–6.

Oberman, Kieran. 2016. "Immigration as a Human

Right." In *Migration in Political Theory: The Ethics of Movement and Membership*, edited by Sarah Fine and Lea Ypi. Oxford University Press.

Office of the Information Commissioner. 2016. *Annual Report, Highlights, 2015/2016*. Government of Canada. www.oic-ci.gc.ca/en/resources/reports-publi cations/2015-2016-1-highlights.

Peonidis, Filimon. 2004. "Does the Suppression of Pro-Terrorist Speech Enhance Collective Security?" In *Ethics of Terrorism & Counter-Terrorism*, edited by Georg Meggle, Andreas Kemmerling and Mark Textor, 319–28. Berlin and Boston: De Gruyter.

Quinn, Ben. 2016. "Nursery 'Raised Fears of Radicalisation over Boy's Cucumber Drawing.'" *The Guardian*, March 11, UK news section. www.the guardian.com/uk-news/2016/mar/11/nursery-radicali sation-fears-boys-cucumber-drawing-cooker-bomb.

Qurashi, Fahid. 2018. "The Prevent Strategy and the UK 'War on Terror': Embedding Infrastructures of Surveillance in Muslim Communities." *Palgrave Communications* 4: 1–13.

Rawlinson, Kevin, and Vikram Dodd. 2019. "Shamima Begum: Isis Briton Faces Move to Revoke Citizenship." *The Guardian*, February 19. www.theguardian.com/ world/2019/feb/19/isis-briton-shamima-begum-to-ha ve-uk-citizenship-revoked.

Rawls, John. 1993. *Political Liberalism*. Columbia University Press.

Reed, Esther D., ed. 2013. *Civil Liberties, National Security and Prospects for Consensus.* Cambridge University Press.

Rehavi, M. Marit, and Sonja B. Starr. 2014. "Racial Disparity in Federal Criminal Sentences." *Journal of Political Economy* 122 (6): 1320–54.

Rights Watch UK. 2016. "Preventing Education? Human Rights and UK Counter-Terrorism Policy in Schools." http://rwuk.org/wp-content/uploads/2016/07/preventing-education-final-to-print-3.compressed-1.pdf.

Risse, Mathias, and Richard Zeckhauser. 2004. "Racial Profiling." *Philosophy & Public Affairs* 32 (2): 131–70.

Ritchie, Hannah, Joe Hasell, Cameron Appel and Max Roser. 2019. "Terrorism." Our World in Data. https://ourworldindata.org/terrorism#which-regions-experience-the-most-terrorism.

Roy van Zuijdewijn, Jeanine de, and Edwin Bakker. 2004. "Returning Western Foreign Fighters: The Case of Afghanistan, Bosnia and Somalia." International Centre for Counter-Terrorism: The Hague. www.icct.nl/download/file/ICCT-De-Roy-van-Zuijdewijn-Bakker-Returning-Western-Foreign-Fighters-June-2014.pdf.

Sabir, Rizwaan. 2016. "Preventing and Countering Violent Extremism through Civil, Political and Human Rights." Submission to the Office of the United Nations High Commissioner of Human Rights. www.ohchr.

org/Documents/Issues/RuleOfLaw/PCVE/Rizwaan_Sa
bir.pdf.

Said, Wadie E. 2014. "Sentencing Terrorist Crimes."
Ohio State Law Journal 75 (3): 477–528.

Scheffler, Samuel. 2006. "Is Terrorism Morally
Distinctive?" *Journal of Political Philosophy* 14 (1):
1–17.

Serwer, Adam. 2019. "The Terrorism That Doesn't
Spark a Panic." *The Atlantic*, January 28. www.theatl
antic.com/ideas/archive/2019/01/homegrown-terroris
ts-2018-were-almost-all-right-wing/581284.

Shue, Henry. 1996. *Basic Rights: Subsistence, Affluence
and U.S. Foreign Policy*. 2nd edn. Princeton University
Press.

START. 2017. "Ideological Motivations of Terrorism in
the United States, 1970–2016." National Consortium
for the Study of Terrorism and Responses to Terrorism,
University of Maryland. www.start.umd.edu/pubs/ST
ART_IdeologicalMotivationsOfTerrorismInUS_Nov
2017.pdf.

Steinhoff, Uwe. 2007. *On the Ethics of War and
Terrorism*. Oxford University Press.

Strickland, Patrick. 2019. "White Nationalism Is an
International Threat." *The New Republic*, March.
https://newrepublic.com/article/153329/white-nationa
lism-international-threat.

Taylor, Isaac. 2018. *The Ethics of Counterterrorism*. New
York: Routledge. www.routledge.com/The-Ethics-

of-Counterterrorism-1st-Edition/Taylor/p/book/9781
138498105.

Thwaites, Rayner. 2016. "New Laws Make Loss
of Citizenship a Counter-Terrorism Tool." *The
Conversation*, December 10. http://theconversation.
com/new-laws-make-loss-of-citizenship-a-counter-terr
orism-tool-51725.

Townshend, Charles. 2002. *Terrorism: A Very Short
Introduction*. Oxford University Press.

UK Home Affairs Committee. 2016. "Radicalisation:
The Counter-Narrative and Identifying the Tipping
Point." Eighth Report of Session 2016–2017. UK:
House of Commons. https://publications.parliament.
uk/pa/cm201617/cmselect/cmhaff/135/135.pdf.

UK Home Office. 2019. "Let's Talk About It – What Is
Prevent?" Let's Talk About It. www.ltai.info/what-is-
prevent.

UK Home Office. 2018. "Individuals Referred to and
Supported through the Prevent Programme, April 2017
to March 2018." https://assets.publishing.service.gov.
uk/government/uploads/system/uploads/attachment_
data/file/763254/individuals-referred-supported-prev
ent-programme-apr2017-mar2018-hosb3118.pdf.

UN Press Release. 2017. "Greater Cooperation Needed
to Tackle Danger Posed by Returning Foreign
Fighters." November 28. www.un.org/press/en/2017/
sc13097.doc.htm.

United Nations. 1948. "Universal Declaration of Human

Rights." www.un.org/en/universal-declaration-human-rights.

von Behr Ines, Anais Reding, Charles Edwards and Luke Gribbon. 2013. "Radicalization in the Digital Age." Rand Europe. www.rand.org/pubs/research_reports/RR453.html.

Waldron, Jeremy. 2003. "Security and Liberty: The Image of Balance." *Journal of Political Philosophy* 11 (2): 191–210. https://doi.org/10.1111/1467-9760.00174.

Waldron, Jeremy. 2006. "Safety and Security." *Nebraska Law Review* 85: 301–53.

Wattad, Mohammed Saif-Alden. 2006. "Is Terrorism a Crime or an Aggravating Factor in Sentencing?" *Journal of International Criminal Justice* 4: 1017–30.

Webb, Adam. 2017. "'Swanning Back In?' Foreign Fighters and the Long Arm of the State." *Citizenship Studies* 21 (3): 291–308.

Weil, Patrick. 2012. *The Sovereign Citizen: Denaturalization and the Origins of the American Republic.* Philadelphia: University of Pennsylvania Press.

Weil, Patrick. 2013. "Citizenship, Passports, and the Legal Identity of Americans: Edward Snowden and Others Have a Case in the Courts." *Yale Law Journal Forum* 123: 565–85.

Whelan, Frederick G. 1981. "Citizenship and the Right to Leave." *American Political Science Review* 75 (3): 636–53.

White, Stuart. 2007. *Equality*. Cambridge: Polity.

Whitt, Matt S. 2017. "Felon Disenfranchisement and Democratic Legitimacy." *Social Theory and Practice* 43 (2): 283–311.

Winter, Tom. 2018. "Boston Marathon Bomber Says It Was Unfair to Try Him in Beantown." *NBC News*, December 27. www.nbcnews.com/news/crime-courts/boston-marathon-bomber-files-appeal-says-judge-erred-keeping-trial-n952451.

Wolfers, Arnold. 1952. "'National Security' as an Ambiguous Symbol." *Political Science Quarterly* 67 (4): 481–502.

Wolff, Jonathan, and Avner de-Shalit. 2007. *Disadvantage*. Oxford University Press.

Wood, Patrick. 2018. "Why Do We Cancel Passports for Terror Suspects – and Not Just Let Them Leave?" *ABC News*, November 20. www.abc.net.au/news/2018-11-21/why-do-we-cancel-passports-for-terror-suspects-and-not-arrest/10517112.